THE ROUTLEDGE

HISTORICAL ATLAS

OF

WOMEN

IN

AMERICA

Routledge Atlases of American History

Series Editor: Mark C. Carnes

THE ROUTLEDGE
HISTORICAL ATLAS
OF
WOMEN
IN
AMERICA

SANDRA OPDYCKE

MARK C. CARNES, SERIES EDITOR

Published in 2000 by
Routledge
29 West 35th Street
New York, NY 10001

Published in Great Britain in 2000 by
Routledge
11 New Fetter Lane
London EC4P 4EE

10 9 8 7 6 5 4 3 2 1

Library of Congress Cataloging-in-Publication Data

Opdycke, Sandra
    The Routledge historical atlas of women in America / Sandra Opdycke.
        p.   cm.—(Routledge atlases of American history)
    Includes bibliographical references and index.
    ISBN 0-415-92132-5 (cloth : alk. paper). — ISBN 0-415-92138-4
    (pbk : alk. paper)
    1. Women—United States—History—Atlases.   I. Title.
    II. Series

HQ1410.P68 2000
973'.082—dc21   99-053346

To Karen

In celebration of her gallant heart and restless feet

Contents

Foreword

"Where are the women?" asks Sandra Opdycke. Her question is directed at the customary historical atlas, whose colorful arrows show the routes by which explorers traversed continents and seas, and armies marched in fateful collision. Her point is that historical atlases, like historians more generally, have focused chiefly on the exploits of men. Her task was to create an historical atlas devoid of the customary features of the genre. What, in fact, is meant by an historical atlas of women?

The pages that follow provide an emphatic and original answer. It not only deepens our understanding of women in American history, but also transforms our conception of an historical atlas.

At first glance, Opdycke's approach may seem familiar. The book proceeds chronologically, beginning with Native American women prior to European contact and ending with women's health and welfare in the 1990s; and her atlas includes the obvious political topics: the progress of the Woman Suffrage Amendment and the defeat of the Equal Rights Amendment; the increase in state and national female legislators after 1973; the advance, by state and over time, of protective legislation such as minimum wage laws for women.

But even a cursory glance suggests how different this historical atlas is from most.

Opdycke perceives that women have not conceived of space solely or even chiefly in terms of political boundaries. The terrain of women's history, she asserts, must be viewed from vastly different perspectives: sometimes, close up, so as to discern discrete figures; sometimes, as from a hill, so as to encompass a neighborhood or community; and sometimes from a great distance, to identify broad state and national trends.

Thus Opdycke examines how individual women moved-literally-out of the home to create and define their own space. One map delineates the world of Rachel Magruder, a slave who was sold and her ten children dispersed over much of Prince George's County from 1755 to 1780. Opdycke follows midwife Martha Ballard, who during three weeks of 1793 repeatedly crossed the frozen Kennebec River to attend to expectant mothers in Hallowell, Maine. Opdycke tracks the indefatigable Eleanor Roosevelt over two years of intense travel, and, decades later, the paths trod by Georganna Deas, an African American community activist who sought to bring medical care to the poor of Brooklyn, New York.

Interior space shaped the lives of American women, so Opdycke ponders a turn-of-the century tenement building, Jane Addams' Hull House, a Japanese internment camp, a postwar house in Levittown, a contemporary fitness center.

Opdycke covers the settlement patterns of frontier and immigrant women, but imparts to these and other subjects yet another layer of meaning. For example, in addition to outlining the exodus of single, African American women from Arkansas, Mississippi and Alabama to Chicago during the early 20th century, she shows how disproportionate numbers of these women settled in particular neighborhoods of Chicago. In a similarly imaginative chapter, Opdycke traces the female employment patterns in twenty Connecticut Valley defense plants during World War II.

Women moved not only across the physical terrain of the nation, but also through imaginative reconstructions of it. Thus Opdycke maps-literally-the Chicago of Theodore Dreiser's fictional protagonist, "Sister Carrie." Opdycke further shows the proliferation of movie theatres in Kansas City in the late 1920s; women figured prominently in this new entertainment medium, both as actors in this fantasy world and as consumers.

A professor of history at Vassar College, Opdycke, the author most recently of *No One Was Turned Away: The Role of Public Hospitals in New York City since 1900* (1999), an exemplary work on the intersection of history and public policy, has now redefined the historical atlas.

Mark C. Carnes
Professor of History
Barnard College, Columbia University

Introduction

Scan a dozen American historical atlases and one important question will come to your mind: Where are the women? Men's achievements are documented on every page: the territories they explored, the railroads they built, the battles they fought, the elections they won. But where are the wives and mothers, the factory girls, the secretaries, the settlement-house workers, the WACs? Where are the women?

This atlas is designed to answer that question. First, it seeks to make more visible the domestic and private sphere in which so many generations of American women lived their lives. Second, it illustrates women's growing presence in the public sphere as volunteers, workers, and citizens. In doing so, it offers a different perspective on the familiar landscape of American history. From the first section, which includes a map of the kind of village where many early Native American women lived their lives, to the last section, which maps the proportion of elderly women by state in 1990, this atlas seeks to illuminate one crucial fact: women have always been part of American history.

Part I, "Breaking Old Ties," deals with the changes and upheavals that women experienced during the early years of American history, up to 1800. For white women from Europe, life in the New World meant separation from friends at home, and then separation again, as settlers kept moving further west. The breaking of ties was still more violent for the thousands of African women transported to America, who lost not only their homes and families but freedom itself. As for Native American women, the growing European presence forced them to give up lands they had occupied for centuries, while precipitating social changes that over time would nearly erase their culture. Finally, at the

Suffrage parades like this one in New York City in 1916 reminded every spectator that, while women served the nation as mothers, they also had political rights that deserved attention.

end of the eighteenth century, the lives of all these women were shaken by another breaking of ties: the American Revolution.

Besides sustaining their families through the many upheavals of colonial life, American women had their own daily work to perform, usually in the role of homemaker. In an era when ready-made commodities were scarce and expensive, housekeeping involved not only child-care and cleaning but also such tasks as spinning, weaving, knitting, gardening, baking, dairying, meat smoking, soap making, and poultry raising. In many Native American tribes the women did all the planting and growing of crops. Even female slaves often found time to garden, cook, and sew for their families. Among white women, the plantation mistress played her role in household production by supervising her slaves and servants, while the more typical farm wife usually did the work on her own or bartered with her neighbors. In every region, the work that women did in their homes represented a vital contribution to the social and economic well-being of the American people.

Part II, "Women's Place in an Expanding Nation" traces the changing patterns of women's lives in the years between 1800 and 1865, a period during which the United States dramatically increased its territory, population, and wealth. Thousands of white families moved westward, Native American families were driven further inland, and immigrants (many from famine-stricken Ireland) flooded into the major ports. Meanwhile, the expanding economy brought new prosperity to the well-off and fostered the emergence of a sizable middle class.

Throughout these years, most American women continued to live on farms and plantations, caring for their families or working as servants or slaves. But the antebellum period did bring important role-changes for some. Yankee farm girls broke new ground by going to work in America's first major factories. Meanwhile, rising incomes, the availability of immigrant servants, and the declining importance of home production combined to give middle- and upper-class women more time for volunteer activities. Many of these women threw themselves into the social movements of the day, crusading for such causes as temperance, child welfare, and the abolition of slavery. Later, during the Civil War, women contributed to the war effort as homemakers and as volunteers. At home, they kept farms and plantations going while their husbands were away. As volunteers they provided both the Union and the Confederacy with indispensable nursing, fund-raising, and supply services.

Part III, "Seeking a Voice," describes how women began to achieve a more independent voice in American society between the Civil War and World War I. Not all women benefited from these changes, of course. It is important to remember the declining position of Native Americans during these years, the southern black women still laboring in the fields they had worked as slaves, the immigrant mothers struggling to make homes for their families in crowded tenements. Despite these difficulties, however, the period between the Civil War and World War I did open new opportunities for many women.

Perhaps the most significant gains were made in the workplace. Nursing, clerical work, and teaching became widely accepted female occupations, and women made their first inroads in such male-dominated fields as law and medicine, art and literature. Industrial jobs also opened up to women in great number; even though most offered poor working conditions, they represented a welcome alternative to the traditional option for women: domestic service. Moreover, female factory workers broke new ground during these years by organizing a series of strikes that drew unprecedented attention to the injustices they faced.

The great majority of women left the workforce when they married, but many remained active in the public sphere as volunteers in the many reform organizations of the period. Other women took that commitment even further by making reform their profession, dedicating their lives to working for better labor conditions, the abolition of child labor, improved public health, and a host of other causes. Overall, the new opportunities that began to open up during these years, and the courage with which many women embraced those opportunities, suggested a range of wider possibilities for the future.

The promises of the early twentieth century remained largely unrealized between 1914 and 1965, as is shown in Part IV, "Two Steps Forward, One Step Back." Nevertheless, certain important gains were made. The winning of suffrage in 1920 qualified women, at least legally, for equal participation in the political life of the nation. Women also joined the Navy and Marines for the first time during World War I, and were accepted into every branch of the military during World War II. Women's participation in these two activities— voting and military service—represented an important step toward the one role that had always eluded them: that of citizen. Women also assumed other new responsibilities during the two world wars—and during the Great Depression as well—holding their families together emotionally and sometimes financially when their husbands were unable to do so.

But each of these periods was followed by a reaction. Even the recognition accorded to female volunteers seemed to wane, compared to the influence that such women wielded during the Depression and in wartime. As for work, once the men were on the job again, women were strongly urged to go back to their traditional role: homemaking. In fact, many women continued to hold jobs, but pictures of happy homemakers dominated the media, effectively denying the daily experience of millions of women. The pervasive images of "typical" suburban housewives during the years after World War II also denied the fact that racial discrimination kept most African-American and Hispanic women out of the suburbs, and that nearly all these women had to work for a living.

Besides receiving little recognition as workers, women had difficulty finding their political voice—a problem that persisted even as late as the early 1960s. By then women had been voting for more than 40 years, yet they generally voted almost exactly the way men did, and a mere handful had been elected to office. Change was in the wind, however. Gradually in the mid-1960s, inspirited by their participation in the civil rights movement and frustrated by the gender discrimination they encountered there, women began to look for ways to assert their own citizenship.

In civil rights demonstrations like the Selma March in 1965, black and white women reached out to each other despite barriers of race and background.

Part V, "Redefining Women's Place," covers the final 45 years of the twentieth century, a period during which every one of the female roles discussed above—homemaker, volunteer, worker, and citizen—underwent significant change. The proportion of women with jobs increased dramatically. Even mothers of very young children joined the workforce in large numbers, sharply reducing the number of young matrons available for volunteer work. But demographic changes produced a new pool of volunteers: retired women. As improvements in medicine and public health enabled women to live longer and healthier lives, many began taking up the volunteer responsibilities that their daughters were too busy to assume.

Meanwhile, the role of homemaker was changing as well; increasingly, homemaking tasks were performed, not by women who regarded them as their life-work, but by women who had already spend a full day doing paid work somewhere else. The persistence of this "double-shift" was a source of stress for many women at all levels of the occupational scale. Nevertheless, women did benefit from the way that work opportunities expanded during the final decades of the twentieth century, opening many fields that had been almost exclusively male domains a generation earlier. Moreover, women themselves played a major role in opening up these opportunities, using their power as citizens to expand their rights as workers. Energized by the women's movement that emerged in the 1960s, they also succeeded in asserting themselves as political candidates, as consumers of health-care, as artists, as businesswomen, and as senior citizens.

Much remained to be done in order to achieve full equality, and even more to ensure that all women had equal access to the gains that were made. But there was an inspiring example to follow: that of the generations of women who had gone before. As homemakers, as volunteers, as workers, and as citizens, these women had helped to build much of what was most valuable in American society. The challenge now was to carry on that tradition, adapting it to the demands of a new century.

PART I: BREAKING OLD TIES:
AMERICAN WOMEN BEFORE 1800

During the years before 1800, hundreds of thousands of women left their old lives behind in Europe or Africa and began building new ones in North America. Once they arrived on the new continent, the process of breaking old ties and constructing new ones continued. Each time a woman and her family left the place they knew to move further west, or a slave watched her husband sold away, or a mother stood over her baby's grave, or one of the recurrent wars took a life or destroyed a village—on each of these occasions, the women involved had to accommodate the loss and start building new lives to replace the old. The ways in which they accomplished these tasks were familiar but essential: They fed and nurtured their families, they preserved the rituals that kept alive their families' connection to the past, and they formed new bonds of love and friendship to replace those that had been broken.

Even Indian women, who had been in America from the start, were forced to go through this process. On the East Coast, the rapid growth of the European colonies pushed the Indians steadily westward, not only into unfamiliar terrain but often into the territory of other tribes. In the Southwest and along the Pacific coast, the Spanish conquest had a similar impact, unsettling Indian life with military raids, religious missions, and forced agricultural labor. Furthermore, all across the North American continent, even among inland tribes that rarely encountered a European face to face, the ways in which Indian women had lived and worked for generations were gradually transformed by the spread of European diseases, trade goods, guns, and horses. Indian society would continue to flourish for many years to come, but the growing pressures on that society were clearly visible by 1800.

African women who were brought to the New World as slaves during these years experienced the most violent dislocation of all. From the arrival of the first slaves in North America in 1619 to the outlawing of importation in 1807, thousands of black women were taken forcibly from their villages. They were then subjected to imprisonment on the African coast, a grim passage across the Atlantic, sale on the auction block in some North American port, and the arduous process of learning to be a slave. Furthermore, even as these women struggled to adapt to their new surroundings, the connections they established were frequently broken again as family and friends were sold away to other masters. Within the iron constraints that surrounded them, female slaves did manage to carve out a space for personal and family life, but no group of American women performed that task under more difficult circumstances.

The white women who came to the New World from Europe had more choice in the matter than the black women brought from Africa, and for some of them, the journey to America represented a welcome chance to start anew, in a freer society than the Old World had offered. Yet nearly all the women who sailed from Europe left behind people and places that were dear to them, and many would probably have chosen to remain at home if they could. Most female convicts, for instance, could be considered voluntary emigrants only in the sense that they preferred a life of exile to death on the gallows. Other women made the trip because poverty or religious oppression made it impossible for them to stay where they were. And perhaps the greatest number—ranging all the way from noblewomen to housemaids—undertook the voyage primarily because the men who made the decisions in their lives had determined that the family should go to America.

In this colonial kitchen, several women (and one elderly man) go about a variety of household tasks: spinning, pie-making, grilling, churning, and keeping an eye on the children.

Having settled in the colonies, these white women encountered still more change and disruption. First, there were the upheavals that most women lived with during these years: epidemics, natural disasters, deaths in the family. Each time one of these cataclysms struck, old connections were broken and it became necessary to build again. A second source of instability was the continual flow of people moving westward. As the population increased and as land along the coast became more expensive, many a colonial family picked up stakes and moved again, or watched their children or their friends set out to find new opportunity along the frontier. Each arrival and departure unsettled old relationships while making new ones possible.

Starting around the middle of the eighteenth century, colonial women experienced a third source of instability: the rupture of the ties between Britain and her North American colonies. The troubled years leading up to the American Revolution caused bitter divisions within colonial society and culminated by breaking one of the most time-honored ties of all: the connection between the king and his subjects. The fight for independence drew many women into unfamiliar roles in political (and sometimes military) affairs, further alienated the patriots from the Indians who sided with the British, exposed thousands of American families to the depredations of war, and drove hundreds of loyalist families into exile. Once the war ended, women's roles were not very different from what they had been before, but the colonial society within which they had performed those roles was replaced by the young republic, and that change presented women with a new set of possibilities and limitations for the future.

For some American women, the repeated breaking of old ties during the years before 1800 represented liberation; for others—especially Indian and black women—it meant loss and dislocation. But as the United States entered the nineteenth century, the country owed much of its vitality to the way in which, despite constant upheavals, women of every race and class had managed to keep weaving and reweaving the social fabric that held together their families and their communities.

The First American Women

For thousands of years, Native American women constituted the entire female population of the territory that would later become the United States. Through most of prehistory, these women lived as members of small bands (usually just a few families) that maintained themselves by some combination of hunting, fishing, and gathering. Starting about 5000 B.C., the development of agriculture made it possible to form larger permanent settlements—villages and even cities. Large parts of the interior were still sparsely inhabited by nomadic bands, but by the time the first Europeans arrived in 1492, the Indians had established significant clusters of population along the Pacific coast, in the Southwest, the Southeast, in the Mississippi Valley, and along the Atlantic coast. Estimates vary, but by that time there were at least 4 million and perhaps as many as 18 million Indians living in North America north of Mexico.

ALEUTS

Like women in many parts of the world, Native American women bore the primary responsibility for the care of their children and for preparing food and clothing. There were, however, two ways in which the lives of Native American women were quite different from those of the European women who would settle on their continent.

For one thing, in Indian society each nuclear family was part of a larger and more important group: the kinship network. The fact that in many communities several families lived under one roof and that many tribes held their land in common reflected a larger idea: that the whole kin network, rather than the nuclear family, was the linchpin of society. As a result, Native American women appear to have had access to a broader set of primary relationships than most European women enjoyed in their nuclear households. The extensive association with female kin probably reached its peak in matrilineal societies such as the Pueblos, the Iroquois, and the Cherokees. In these places, it was the men rather than the women who moved to their spouses' communities when they married; thus it was the women who remained in the community from generation to generation, maintaining the continuity of the tribe through their daughters and granddaughters.

This drawing suggests what an Indian village in North Carolina might have looked like, several hundred years before the European settlers began to arrive.

A second major difference between the lives of Native American and European women lay in the fact that in most agricultural areas Indian women did virtually all the field labor, while men performed the tasks that required being away from the village: hunting, fishing, trading, fighting, and treaty making. Contemporary European observers often criticized

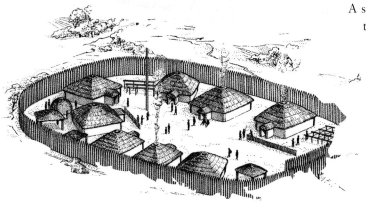

this arrangement, maintaining that Indian men were lazy and their women overworked. Yet the women's vital role in providing food gave them higher community standing than most European women enjoyed. In many tribes, women had a considerable voice in religious or political affairs, and among some peoples such as the Pueblo, Hopi, Zuni, and Iroquois, women actually owned the fields collectively and controlled how the food was distributed.

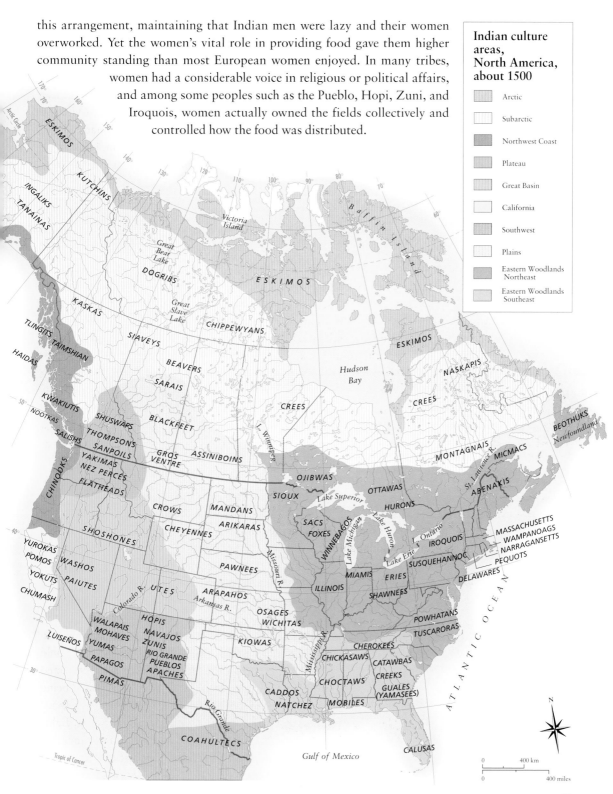

Indian culture areas, North America, about 1500

- Arctic
- Subarctic
- Northwest Coast
- Plateau
- Great Basin
- California
- Southwest
- Plains
- Eastern Woodlands Northeast
- Eastern Woodlands Southeast

European Women in the New World

During the early 1600s, English women helped establish the first two permanent European colonies in the future United States—one in Jamestown, Virginia, and the other in Plymouth, Massachusetts. Thousands more Europeans followed, as well as a growing number of African slaves. By 1700 there were about 250,000 people in the American colonies, of whom just over 10 percent were black.

Most white female colonists of the seventeenth century, whether in the North or the South, worked as farmers' wives, presiding over a continual round of tasks involved in feeding, clothing, and caring for their families. Black women, too, generally worked on farms and oversaw the preparation of food and clothes for their families. None of these women could vote, hold church office, make a contract, or own property if she were married. Yet beyond the similarities they shared, colonial women's lives did differ by region, as can be seen if we compare the experience in Virginia and Massachusetts.

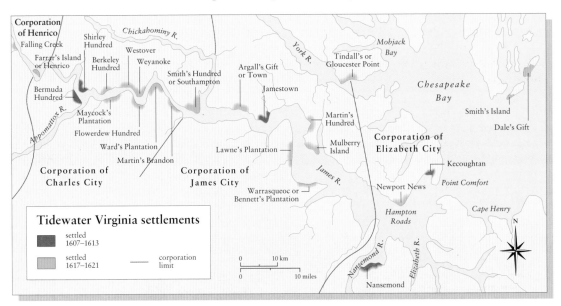

Tidewater Virginia settlements

settled 1607–1613

settled 1617–1621

corporation limit

0   10 km
0   10 miles

The first two women arrived in Jamestown, Virginia, in 1608, a year after the colony's founding. Since supplies from England arrived erratically and the colonists were reluctant farmers, only the Indians' generosity kept them alive during the first difficult years. Tobacco growing emerged as Virginia's salvation, and within a few decades it attracted a flood of new immigrants from Europe. Many of the female newcomers were indentured servants, bound to six or seven years of labor. They found themselves in a society divided by growing economic inequality, shadowed by a death rate higher than the worst epidemic years in England, and moving toward a dependence on slave labor. Yet despite its problems, Virginia promised these women a better life than at home, including plenty of marriage offers when their indentures were up, since for many years the colony had far more men than women.

A thousand miles away in Massachusetts, the Puritans were also facing challenges, but after a desperate first winter in 1620–1621, they moved more quickly than Virginia to a condition of relative stability. For one thing, most of the Puritans immigrated in family groups, which made for a more settled community life. In addition, because most of the Puritan couples came intending to work as farmers, food shortages were rare. (This, plus a more familiar climate, may help explain why life expectancy in Massachusetts was over 70 years, compared to under 50 in Virginia.) Finally, New England's very drawbacks—its stony soil and harsh winters—saved Massachusetts from two factors that kept life in Virginia unsettled: the continual influx of new immigrants and the emergence of large plantations that lent themselves to slave labor.

One more thing distinguished Massachusetts from Virginia. In Massachusetts, most settlers lived close together in towns. This could involve women in the petty conflicts of small-town life, but it also gave them regular opportunities to see friends, go to church, and exchange services with neighbors. In Virginia, where families generally lived on separate plantations, women spent much more of their time within the circle of their own households and had less opportunity to benefit from the conversation and support of other wives.

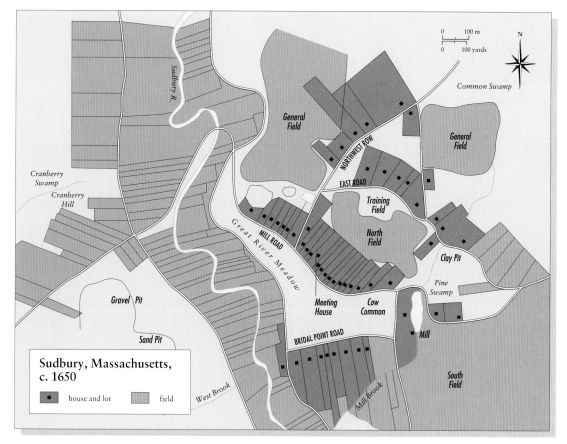

Sudbury, Massachusetts, c. 1650

Women in the Northern Colonies

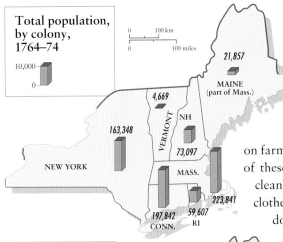

Total population, by colony, 1764–74

10,000

0

21,857

MAINE (part of Mass.)

4,669

NH

VERMONT

163,348

73,097

NEW YORK

MASS.

223,841

197,842 59,607

CONN. RI

Between 1700 and 1780, the population of the American colonies increased more than tenfold, from 250,000 to nearly 3 million. Driving that increase were two important trends: soaring levels of immigration, and a rising standard of living that fostered long lives and bigger families.

Nearly all female colonists in the North lived on farms and most pursued similar duties. People spoke of these tasks as "indoor" work, but besides cooking, cleaning, washing, spinning, weaving, and making clothes, candles, and soap, there were a number of outdoor chores that were classified as women's work, including keeping the family garden, tending pigs and chickens, smoking and salting meat, and milking the cows. The average female colonist also bore and cared for six to eight children in the course of her life.

Community events like barn raisings provided occasional opportunities to socialize, but farm wives and their daughters spent most of their time close to home, tied down by difficult travel conditions, the continuous labor of agricultural life, and the gender distinctions that excluded women from the public worlds of trading, litigation, and politics.

Urban life offered women in the northern colonies a somewhat broader range of opportunities, particularly

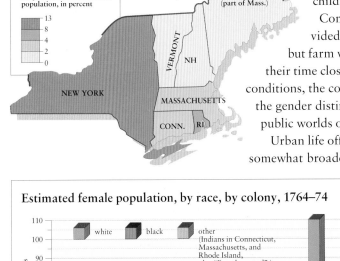

Black population, by colony, 1764–74

Proportion of blacks in total population, in percent

13
8
4
2
0

MAINE (part of Mass.)

VERMONT

NH

NEW YORK

MASSACHUSETTS

CONN. RI

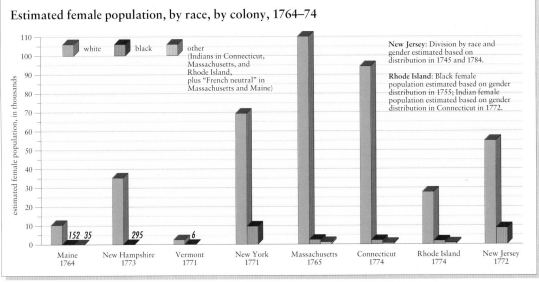

Estimated female population, by race, by colony, 1764–74

estimated female population, in thousands

white   black   other
(Indians in Connecticut, Massachusetts, and Rhode Island, plus "French neutral" in Massachusetts and Maine)

New Jersey: Division by race and gender estimated based on distribution in 1745 and 1784.

Rhode Island: Black female population estimated based on gender distribution in 1755; Indian female population estimated based on gender distribution in Connecticut in 1772.

152 35   295   6

Maine 1764   New Hampshire 1773   Vermont 1771   New York 1771   Massachusetts 1765   Connecticut 1774   Rhode Island 1774   New Jersey 1772

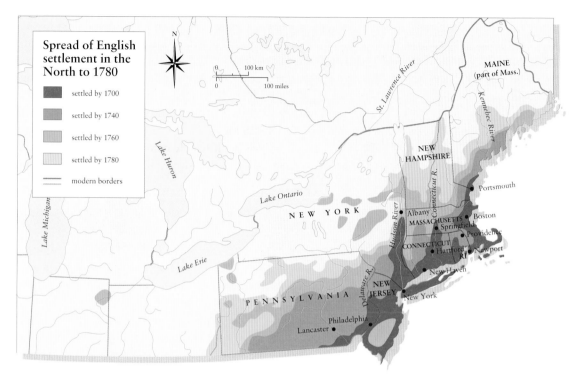

in British America's three largest cities: Philadelphia, New York, and Boston. Like farm women, urban housewives produced many of the goods that their families consumed, and they often added to the household income by making extra food or clothes for sale. But in addition, urban wives frequently played a role in their husbands' businesses, since city craftsmen and small merchants usually maintained their shops in their homes. If a woman were single or widowed, she might support herself by working as a maid, laundress, cook, seamstress, or nurse, by opening a boardinghouse or small shop, or by apprenticing to become a midwife or milliner. When all else failed, urban women could turn to prostitution.

City life was much less healthy than the country. For mothers, perhaps the most painful indicator of this was the fact that only half the children born in cities lived to the age of 21. Urban areas were also characterized by greater and more visible extremes of wealth and poverty; one was much more likely to see a grande dame in her carriage or a widow begging for food on a city street than in some country town. On the positive side, city life made housekeeping somewhat easier, since some household goods could be purchased ready-made. There was also the chance to socialize with neighbors and to enjoy the high or low culture of the urban community. Taken together, cities accounted for only 4 percent of the colonial population, and none contained more than 25,000 people by 1775. Yet they had disproportional impact socially and economically, and they represented a broader range of experiences—for better and for worse—than most women encountered in the country.

Women in the Southern Colonies

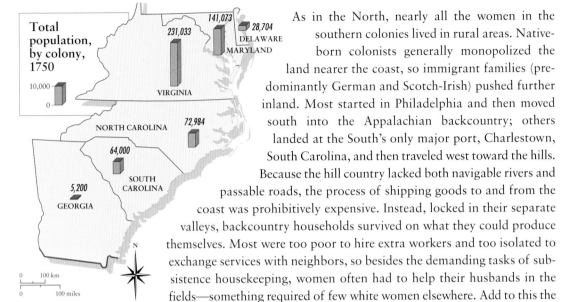

Total population, by colony, 1750

141,073
231,033
28,704
DELAWARE
MARYLAND
10,000
0
VIRGINIA
NORTH CAROLINA 72,984
64,000
5,200
SOUTH CAROLINA
GEORGIA
N
0   100 km
0   100 miles

Black population, by colony, 1750

Proportion of blacks in total population, in percent

61
37
23
10
0

VIRGINIA
DEL.
MARYLAND
NORTH CAROLINA
SOUTH CAROLINA
GEORGIA

As in the North, nearly all the women in the southern colonies lived in rural areas. Native-born colonists generally monopolized the land nearer the coast, so immigrant families (predominantly German and Scotch-Irish) pushed further inland. Most started in Philadelphia and then moved south into the Appalachian backcountry; others landed at the South's only major port, Charlestown, South Carolina, and then traveled west toward the hills. Because the hill country lacked both navigable rivers and passable roads, the process of shipping goods to and from the coast was prohibitively expensive. Instead, locked in their separate valleys, backcountry households survived on what they could produce themselves. Most were too poor to hire extra workers and too isolated to exchange services with neighbors, so besides the demanding tasks of subsistence housekeeping, women often had to help their husbands in the fields—something required of few white women elsewhere. Add to this the periodic conflict with Indians and the isolation of a region in which the nearest church or store might be a day's ride away, and one can appreciate the hard life that women faced on the eighteenth-century frontier.

Women who lived on plantations near the coast led very different lives. South Carolina offered the most extreme contrast to the backcountry, thanks to the emergence of rice in the 1690s as an enormously profitable staple crop. The implications for black women are discussed in the next section, but the fortunes that white planters earned from rice gave their wives and daughters a life of luxury unequaled north of the Caribbean. Spending the hot summer months in their Charlestown mansions, then moving to their baronial plantations when the weather cooled, the planters' wives did have responsibility for supervising their elaborate households, yet the contrast with the hard-pressed women of the frontier could hardly be greater.

The plantations of Virginia, North Carolina, and Maryland were less grand than those in South Carolina, but they too were quite prosperous. Throughout the coastal areas of the Upper South, rising tobacco prices and an expanding variety of other crops built a solid class of wealthy landowners and a considerable number of comfortable small planters. Women who lived on these plantations had far better access than backcountry women to manufactured goods and social gatherings. Nevertheless, towns in the southern colonies were few and far between, and these women still spent much of

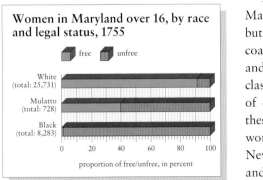

Women in Maryland over 16, by race and legal status, 1755

free   unfree

White (total: 25,731)
Mulatto (total: 728)
Black (total: 8,283)

0   20   40   60   80   100
proportion of free/unfree, in percent

their lives within the circle of their own immediate families.

Whether the plantation mistress lived in the Upper or Lower South, she was responsible, like most rural women, for ensuring that the members of her household were kept fed, clothed, and healthy. (This often included some level of responsibility for the welfare of the family's servants and slaves.) Because of the greater wealth on the coast, the greater availability of indentured servants, and the growing importation of slaves, the plantation mistress did less physical labor than the typical frontier farm wife. Nevertheless, she carried the serious—and for some women truly daunting—responsibility of working through her servants to maintain a comfortable and smooth-running household.

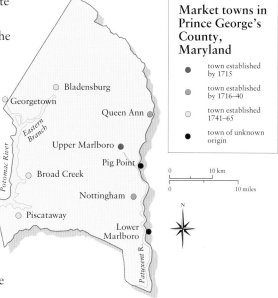

Market towns in Prince George's County, Maryland

- town established by 1715
- town established by 1716–40
- town established 1741–65
- town of unknown origin

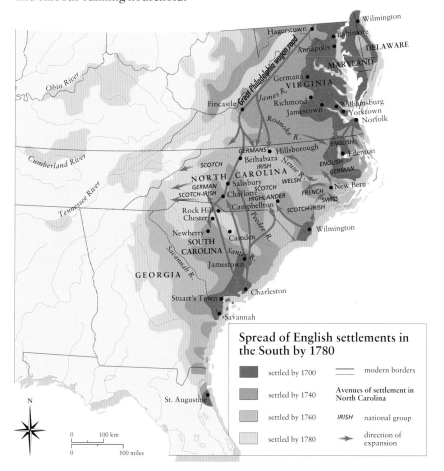

Spread of English settlements in the South by 1780

- settled by 1700
- settled by 1740
- settled by 1760
- settled by 1780

modern borders

Avenues of settlement in North Carolina

IRISH national group

direction of expansion

Enslaved Women in the Colonies

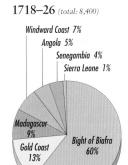

Origin of African slaves entering Port York, Virginia, 1718–39

1718–26 *(total: 8,400)*

- Windward Coast 7%
- Angola 5%
- Senegambia 4%
- Sierra Leone 1%
- Madagascar 9%
- Gold Coast 13%
- Bight of Biafra 60%

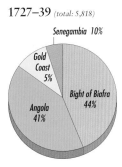

1727–39 *(total: 5,818)*

- Senegambia 10%
- Gold Coast 5%
- Angola 41%
- Bight of Biafra 44%

During the first half of the eighteenth century, roughly 150,000 Africans were brought to the American colonies against their will. Seized by force, mainly in West Africa, they endured appalling conditions on the voyage to the New World and then, on their arrival, were sold into slavery.

Most American slaves were bought by southern planters along the coast; few backcountry farmers could afford them, and because the kind of agriculture practiced in the North did not lend itself to large groups of year-round laborers, the northern colonies accounted for only about 15 percent of the total enslaved population. By 1750, blacks outnumbered whites in South Carolina. They represented perhaps 20 percent of the population in Georgia, about 40 percent in the Chesapeake region, and only about 14 percent in New York, the northern colony with the largest proportion of slaves.

Since the North American mainland accounted for only a small fraction of the entire New World slave trade, mainland planters were often outbid for the most coveted type of slave, the young male. Accordingly, a much larger proportion of North American slaves were women. This helped to humanize the system somewhat, even though it happened by default, because it made it easier for slaves to form families and social networks. Virtually everywhere else in the New World, masters had to use constant importation simply to offset the losses caused by high death rates and the lack of children. In the North American colonies, the rate of natural increase was so great that the slave population expanded steadily, even though imports declined after mid-century.

The experience of enslaved women varied significantly from place to place. In northern towns, black women often worked as domestic servants. Along the Chesapeake, they typically worked in the fields on plantations containing an

John Antrobus' 1860 painting of a night-time burial reflects what an important part religious ceremony played in the slaves' spiritual and social lives.

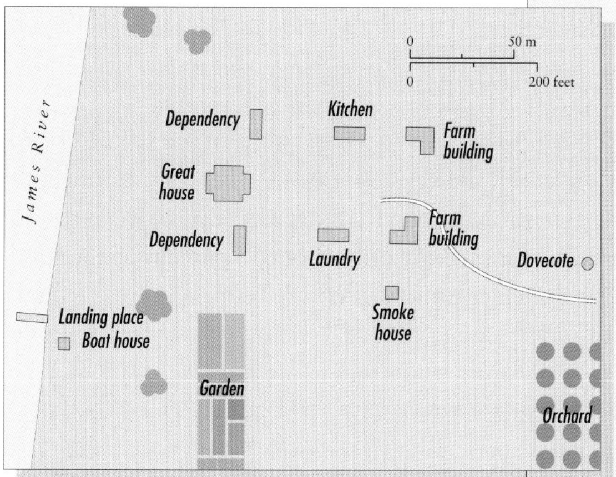

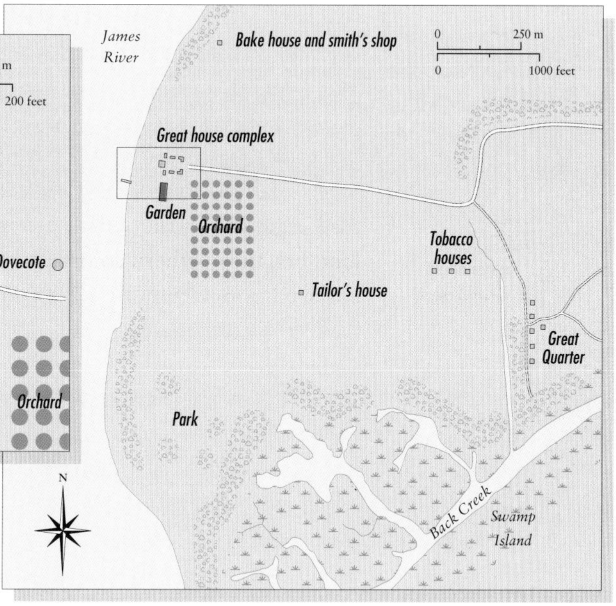

A plantation in Virginia, 1742

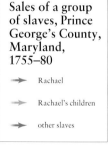

average of 10 or 20 slaves. In the rice country of South Carolina, as many as 50 male and female slaves might labor on a single plantation. In general, the conditions of slavery were considerably harsher in South Carolina, but the masters' reluctance to linger in the malarial climate did produce the "task system," which gave the slaves almost total control over the way they did their work, so long as their assigned tasks were completed.

When work for the master was done, enslaved women went home to their families. On southern plantations, they usually lived in a cluster of huts like the "Great Quarter" in the accompanying plantation map. There the women cooked and sewed for their families, cared for their children, and sometimes raised gardens and kept chickens to supplement the family diet. They perpetuated African traditions of music, dance, storytelling, and religion. At the same time, they struggled to resist—and, if necessary, to survive—the recurrent dangers of physical punishment, of being separated from those they loved, of sexual predation by whites, and of despair over a life of captivity. Despite primitive housing, meager food, and a lifetime of labor (including during pregnancy), slave women played a vital role in establishing the foundations of the black community in America.

Sales of a group of slaves, Prince George's County, Maryland, 1755–80

Rachael
Rachael's children
other slaves

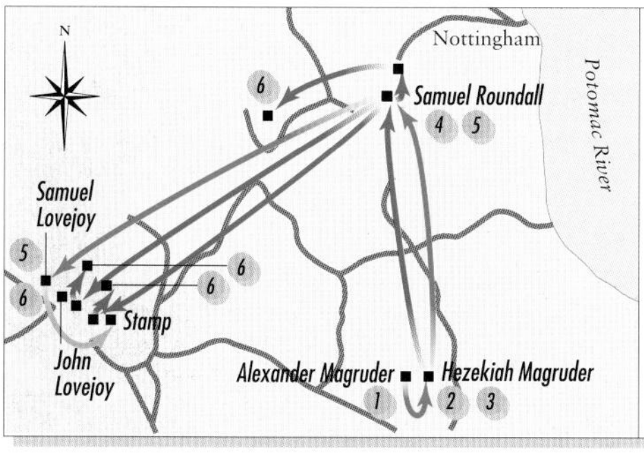

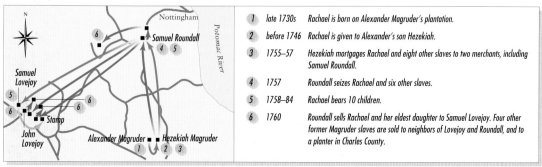

1	late 1730s	Rachael is born on Alexander Magruder's plantation.
2	before 1746	Rachael is given to Alexander's son Hezekiah.
3	1755–57	Hezekiah mortgages Rachael and eight other slaves to two merchants, including Samuel Roundall.
4	1757	Roundall seizes Rachael and six other slaves.
5	1758–84	Rachael bears 10 children.
6	1760	Roundall sells Rachael and her eldest daughter to Samuel Lovejoy. Four other former Magruder slaves are sold to neighbors of Lovejoy and Roundall, and to a planter in Charles County.

Women in the Revolutionary Era

The American Revolution, as well as the contentious years leading up to it, opened new opportunities for colonial women to take part in public life. So long as control of the colonies' affairs lay within established political structures, both law and tradition dictated that men alone would participate. But the politics of colonial resistance demanded a wider arena and a more diverse cast of characters. Looking outside the established institutions, all of which were tied to England, the patriot leaders took their allies where they could find them—in the streets, taverns, parlors, marketplaces, and workshops of everyday society—and many of those allies were women.

Starting in the late 1760s, Parliament passed a series of acts setting new duties on items such as sugar, linen, paper, and tea. Women were soon called upon to help mobilize a boycott against the contested goods, which the patriots saw as unjustly taxed. The female colonists not only stopped using the products, but transformed private acts into public ones by formally affirming the political meaning of their actions. "Tea I have not drunk since last Christmas, nor bought a new gown," wrote one woman. "I know this, that as free I can die but once, but as a slave I shall not be worthy of life." In Boston, a group of 300 female patriots pledged to drink no tea and explained that they were doing so to "save this abused Country from Ruin and Slavery."

To support the boycott against imported fabric, many colonial women organized huge and well-publicized spinning bees, and made it a patriotic point to wear dresses made of homespun. In some places, these neighborhood circles evolved into formal organizations, often called Daughters of Liberty to stress their support for their fiery male counterparts, the Sons of Liberty. Although neither spinning nor the choice of an afternoon beverage moved women into particularly contested gender territory, their interpretation of these acts in political terms represented a new departure.

Once the fighting began in 1775, both patriot and loyalist women supported their chosen sides. Most did so in ways that were traditional for women in wartime—managing family affairs while their husbands were away, knitting socks for the soldiers, collecting money and supplies, bringing food to the hungry troops, and keeping house for billeted officers. Perhaps 20,000 women traveled with the two armies; some worked as cooks, nurses, laundresses, and prostitutes, while most simply cared for their own soldier husbands. In addition, many women played more adventurous roles—spying for one side or the other, carrying messages in and out of besieged towns, hiding and nursing fugitives, smuggling supplies through enemy lines, taking a hand with a cannon at crucial moments, or dressing themselves as men and serving as soldiers.

Women did not achieve equal status in revolutionary society, and the small ground they gained was mostly lost in the postrevolutionary years. Nevertheless, they played an important part in the fight for independence, and the rhetoric of liberty and self-determination that was articulated during the prewar years would echo again in the women's rights convention at Seneca Falls 70 years later.

Women's participation in the Revolution

- ■ boycotting British goods
- ■ using physical force against the enemy
- ▪ providing money, food, supplies, and nursing care
- ■ providing clandestine information or assistance

VERMONT

- ■ West Salisbury: Widow Ann Story spies on local loyalists for the patriot Green Mountain Boys.

MASSACHUSETTS

- ■ Boston: In 1769, 28 newspaper articles appear in six months describing female resistance to British import taxes.
- ■ Women organize "mass spinning bees" in 1769 to demonstrate their resistance to using British cloth.
- ■ Boston: Hundreds of women support the boycott of imported tea in 1770.
- ■ Boston: In 1774, women tar and feather the wife and daughter of man who has joined the British army.
- ■ Groton: Armed village women capture British soldiers who are retreating from Lexington in 1775.
- ■ Pepperell: Female militia, dressed as men, ambush a British spy in 1775 and turn him over to the patriots.
- ■ Boston: Deborah Champion & Sarah Fulton smuggle messages through British lines to patriots in Cambridge.
- ■ Deborah Sampson fights in the army dressed as a man; she serves gallantly from 1781 to 1783.

RHODE ISLAND

- ■ Newport: To dramatize their boycott of British imports, 70 ladies gather to spin their own thread.

CONNECTICUT

- ■ Guilford: Agnes Lee scares off approaching British soldiers by firing a cannon to warn her neighbors.
- ▪ Litchfield: Women use the statue of King George III, pulled down by patriots in New York City, to make 42,000 cartridges.

NEW YORK

- ■ Long Island: Local women organize mass spinning bees to support the nonimportation cause.
- ■ New York City: For serving as a courier to the British, Lorenda Holmes has her feet burned by the patriots.
- ■ New York City: At Fort Tryon in 1776, Margaret Corbin fills in for her wounded husband at the cannon.
- ■ New York City: As Mary Murray's hospitality distracts British gènerals, 4,000 patriot troops escape the city.
- ■ Poughkeepsie: When a band of loyalist guerrillas is arrested, five of the members turn out to be women.
- ■ Carmel: 16-year-old Sybil Ludington rides 40 miles to notify the local militia of a British attack nearby.
- ■ Albany: Catherine Schuyler burns her family wheat fields to deny them to the British; neighbors do the same.
- ■ Long Island: The Culper Ring, mainly women, warns the patriots of British patrols on Long Island Sound.
- ■ New York City: Elizabeth Burgin helps patriot prisoners escape from the occupied city.
- ▪ New York City: A group of female loyalists buys a ship and outfits it as a privateer to harass the patriot fleet.

NEW JERSEY

- ▪ Learning of the soldiers' bleeding feet, Rhoda Farrand organizes her neighbors to knit hundreds of socks.
- ■ Freehold: At the Battle of Monmouth, Mary Hays takes her fallen husband's place firing the cannon.
- ▪ New Jersey women help raise funds for the patriot troops.
- ■ Newark: Surrounded by Hessians, Ann Plume manages to capture one and turn him over to the patriots.

PENNSYLVANIA

- ▪ Philadelphia: Esther Reed establishes the "Association," a national fund-raising network for the patriots.
- ■ Valley Forge: Milliner Margaret Hutchinson and teacher Ann Bates spy on the patriot camp for the British.
- ▪ Valley Forge: Mary Frazier tirelessly collects and sews clothes for the patriot soldiers in winter quarters.
- ■ Philadelphia: While British General Howe is billeted in her house, Lydia Darragh spies on him for the patriots.

DELAWARE

- ■ Delaware women help to raise funds to buy clothes and supplies for the patriot troops.

MARYLAND

- ▪ Maryland women organize local fund-raising to improve conditions for the patriot troops.
- ■ Baltimore: While Fort McHenry is under attack in 1782, Betty Zane dashes out and brings back gun powder.

VIRGINIA

- ▪ Williamsburg: Local women form an association in 1773 to boycott East India tea.
- ■ Virginia women help raise funds for the patriot troops.

NORTH CAROLINA

- ■ Edenton: In 1774, 51 women pledge to boycott tea and English cloth until the Townshend Acts are repealed.
- ▪ Greensboro: When her son is wounded, Kerenhappuch Turner rides 300 miles to nurse him on the battlefield.
- ▪ Salisbury: Tavern owner Elizabeth Steele donates her life savings to help the patriot army recruit soldiers.
- ■ High Point: Quaker Hannah Millikan Blair risks her life hiding patriot soldiers from the British.

SOUTH CAROLINA

- ■ South Carolina women publicly urge the women of Virginia and Pennsylvania to resist luxury imports, "especially tea."
- ■ Clinton: Mary Musgrove smuggles food and information to a patriot leader who is hiding from the British.
- ■ Lexington: Emily Geiger carries messages for the patriots through 100 miles of British-occupied countryside.
- ■ 15-year-old Dicey Langston spies for the patriots on British troops occupying her father's farm.
- ▪ Charleston: Women in the occupied city hide food under their clothes and deliver it to the patriot army.
- ■ Spartanburg: Learning of an impending British attack, Kate Moore rides off to rouse the countryside.
- ▪ Women organize to raise funds for the patriot troops.

GEORGIA

- ■ Ann Gwinnett writes to inform Congress that the local patriot soldiers are loyal, but their officers are not.
- ■ Elberton: Caught by British soldiers, Nancy Hart shoots one and holds the rest at bay until help arrives.

Proclamation Line, 1763

West Salisbury
VERMONT
NEW HAMPSHIRE
Pepperell
Lexington
Groton
Albany
MASS. Boston
CONN. RI
Litchfield Guilford Newport
NEW YORK
Poughkeepsie
Carmel
New York
Newark Freehold
PENNSYLVANIA
Philadelphia
Valley Forge NEW JERSEY
DELAWARE
Baltimore
MARYLAND
VIRGINIA
Williamsburgh
Edenton
Greensboro
High Point NORTH CAROLINA
Salisbury
Spartanburg
Clinton Lexington
SOUTH CAROLINA
Charleston
Elberton
GEORGIA

0   100 km
0   100 miles
N

Women in the Young Republic

The years following the American Revolution brought little change in women's status. One might have thought that the egalitarian republicanism propounded during the revolution would have opened the door to greater autonomy for women. But in fact, that philosophy helped to justify the status quo between the genders—and between the races—because it placed great emphasis on a citizen's capacity to make free and independent judgments. Since both women and slaves were legally and economically subordinate, it was argued, they could not possibly participate as equals in the life of the republic. Nor did the practical value of women's contributions during the revolutionary decade win them new consideration, perhaps in part because so many of their efforts— such as providing food and clothing to the troops, spinning, and boycotting household goods—appeared to lie within the traditional "women's sphere." Writing in 1776, Abigail Adams urged her husband John Adams to "Remember the Ladies" when writing laws for the new republic, but the years that followed brought few changes along those lines.

Instead of gaining new independence, women were encouraged to think freshly about the political importance of carrying out their traditional roles as wives and mothers. They were not simply serving their families, it was explained; they were serving the nation

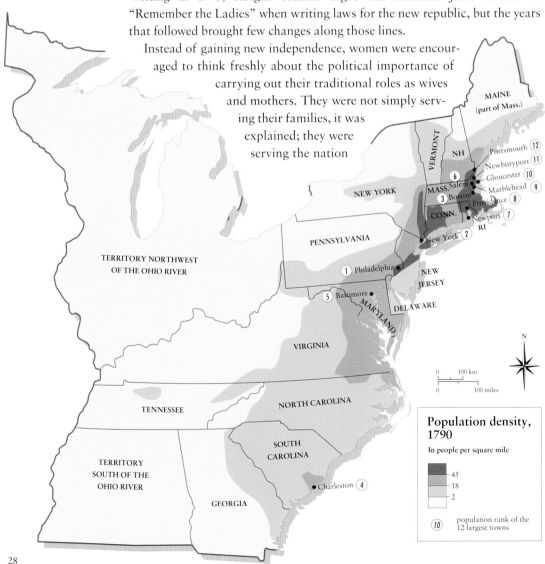

MAINE
(part of Mass.)

VERMONT

NH

Portsmouth ⑫
Newburyport ⑪
Gloucester ⑩

⑥
MASS. Salem
Marblehead ⑨

NEW YORK

③ Boston
Providence ⑧

CONN.
Newport ⑦
RI

New York ②

PENNSYLVANIA

① Philadelphia

NEW
JERSEY

TERRITORY NORTHWEST
OF THE OHIO RIVER

⑤ Baltimore

DELAWARE

MARYLAND

VIRGINIA

N

0   100 km

0   100 miles

TENNESSEE

NORTH CAROLINA

TERRITORY
SOUTH OF THE
OHIO RIVER

SOUTH
CAROLINA

Charleston ④

GEORGIA

Population density, 1790

In people per square mile

	45
	18
	2

⑩   population rank of the
      12 largest towns

by nurturing a new generation of citizens. "Republican motherhood" was thus defined as the way for women to make their patriotic contribution to the nation. This conceptualization brought few changes in the general pattern of women's lives, but it did produce one important reform: a considerable expansion of female education. Not only were public schools increasingly opened to girls as well as boys, but also many private academies were founded to give further training to girls who could afford it. Although colleges remained closed to women, these new initiatives did represent a national commitment to the idea that women in the new nation needed sufficient grounding to raise their children as educated citizens. It also kept alive the possibility that girls raised to be republican mothers might use their education to raise broader questions in the future.

The exclusion of women from political and economic power helped resolve a problem that troubled many male patriots: the tension between the community-minded republicanism that had infused the revolutionary years and the more individualistic values that were in fact emerging as market capitalism took root in American society. Women, because of their separation from the market, could carry on the old values, promoting humanitarianism through family life and philanthropy, while their husbands sought success in the marketplace. To a considerable extent this model was followed, providing the philosophical basis for a dramatic increase in women's charitable activities, especially in the nation's growing cities, where poverty was most acute and most visible. The argument left unaddressed, however, the question of whether a society could live by two sets of values pursued on such unequal terms, and what would happen to the many women who could not afford the luxury of devoting themselves to republican motherhood.

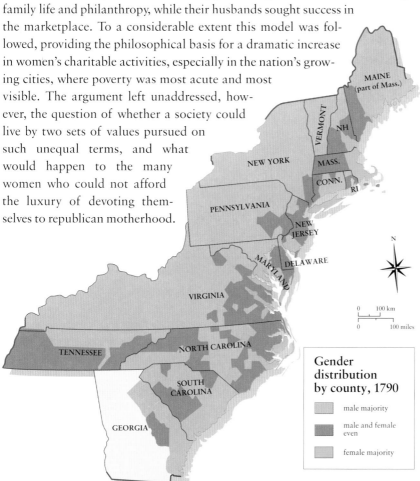

Gender distribution by county, 1790

- male majority
- male and female even
- female majority

Martha Ballard, Eighteenth-Century Midwife

Martha Ballard's diary, 1793:

"Nov. 18: At Capt Meloys. His Lady in Labour. Her women Calld (it was a sever storm of rain. Cleard of with snow). My patient delivered at 8 hour 5 minute Evening of a fine daughter. Her attendants Mrss Cleark, Duttun, Sewall, & myself. We had an Elligant supper and I tarried all night.

Nov. 19: Clear. I returnd home after dineing. Revd Mr Turner and Esq Cony supt here. I was Calld to Mr Parkers at 11 Evening."

from Laurel Ulrich, *A Midwife's Tale*

On December 7, 1793, a midwife named Martha Ballard sat down in Hallowell, Maine, to record the day's events. She wrote: "At Whites. His wife was deliverd at 12 O Clock of a daughter and I was Calld back to Mr Parkers. His Lady was delivrd at 9 hour 30 minutes of a daughter. I am some fatagud. Son Town here." We know what happened that December day because of three remarkable occurrences. First, Ballard maintained a daily record of her activities, not just in 1793 but for 27 years. Second, the women in her family preserved her diary, handing it down from generation to generation. Third, the historian Laurel Thatcher Ulrich recognized the diary's significance and published a book about it, *A Midwife's Tale*. Thus a female chain spanning two centuries has provided us with a rare window on the lives of rural women during the final years of the eighteenth century.

Like many women of her era, Ballard married at 19, bore nine children in 23 years, and lost three of them to childhood diseases. She moved with her family to Hallowell, a town on the Maine frontier, when she was 43, and did not start her diary until 1785, when she was 50. But she remained in excellent health, and her daily entries help us understand the many tasks for which women were responsible. Besides cooking, washing, cleaning, sewing, spinning, dairying, and gardening for their own families, most women used their individual skills to produce additional goods for barter or sale: textiles, garments, honey, baked goods, and so on. Ballard's skill was weaving—a process she would start by trading for the flax or wool that a neighbor had produced, and complete by exchanging the finished cloth for other home-produced goods, for cash, or sometimes for credit at the general store. This busy commerce among Ballard and her female neighbors represented an important sector of the town's economy.

Besides their economic role, Ballard and the other women of Hallowell took the lead in ensuring that their community's social needs were met. Even a practice as simple as their frequent visiting helped sustain the social fabric. In addition, women were the ones who assisted each other in childbirth, nursed the sick, sat with the dying, bathed the dead, and cared for the children of absent or ailing parents. Ballard was particularly important in the town's system of social services because she was a midwife. Although the town's male doctors were occasionally called in to consult, Ballard and a few other midwives delivered nearly all local babies and also treated many sick neighbors.

During the years she kept her diary, Ballard presided over more than 800 births. Her daily entries help us understand what that work entailed. Many was the time she fought her way across the Kennebec River in ice and storm to deliver an expected baby, waited for hours and sometimes days in vain, returned home, then repeated the difficult passage several times more before the baby finally made its appearance. Ballard took the long delays in her stride, noting placidly that one baby's slow arrival had given her time to knit two pairs of gloves and five and a half pairs of mittens. She also described her travel difficulties with verve. "I Crost the stream on the way on fleeting Loggs & got safe

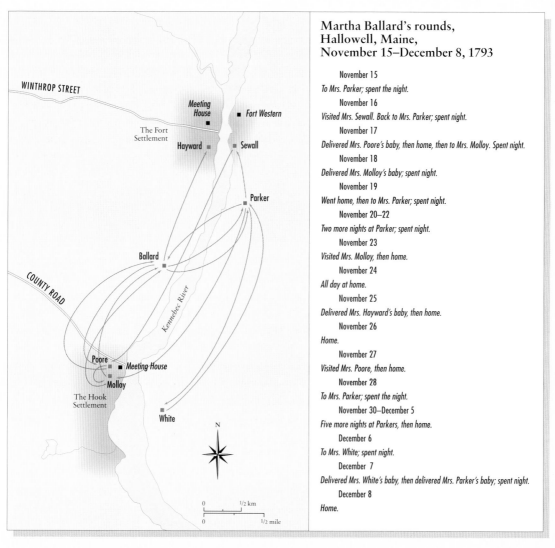

Martha Ballard's rounds, Hallowell, Maine, November 15–December 8, 1793

November 15
To Mrs. Parker; spent the night.
November 16
Visited Mrs. Sewall. Back to Mrs. Parker; spent night.
November 17
Delivered Mrs. Poore's baby, then home, then to Mrs. Molloy. Spent night.
November 18
Delivered Mrs. Molloy's baby; spent night.
November 19
Went home, then to Mrs. Parker; spent night.
November 20–22
Two more nights at Parker; spent night.
November 23
Visited Mrs. Molloy, then home.
November 24
All day at home.
November 25
Delivered Mrs. Hayward's baby, then home.
November 26
Home.
November 27
Visited Mrs. Poore, then home.
November 28
To Mrs. Parker; spent the night.
November 30–December 5
Five more nights at Parkers, then home.
December 6
To Mrs. White; spent night.
December 7
Delivered Mrs. White's baby, then delivered Mrs. Parker's baby; spent night.
December 8
Home.

over," she wrote on one occasion. "A Larg tree blew up by the roots before me which Caused my hors to spring back & my life was spared. Great & marvillous are they sparing mercies O God. I was assisted over the fallen tree by Mr Hains. Went on. Soon Came to a stream. The Bridg was gone. Mr Hewin took the rains waded thro & led the horse. Assisted by the same allmighty power I got safe thro & arrived unhurt."

Each time Ballard sallied forth, she was simultaneously earning income for her family, functioning as part of the local health system, providing support to a neighbor, and pursuing a satisfying profession. Hearing her voice across the centuries, we respond to her energy and distinctive accomplishments. But her diary achieves a larger purpose; its picture of life in one small Maine town helps us understand better the role that thousands of eighteenth-century women played in the lives of their communities.

PART II: WOMEN'S PLACE IN AN EXPANDING NATION: 1800–1865

Between 1800 and 1865, the United States tripled in size, and the country's western boundary moved all the way from the Mississippi River to the Pacific coast. Women were deeply involved in this process of national expansion. For Indian women, the growth of white settlement meant a continuation of the forced moves westward that had begun during colonial times; by 1860 there was virtually no Indian territory left east of the Mississippi River, and most of the resettled tribes were living on the Great Plains. Meanwhile, as the Indians were being forced out, white women had begun crossing the Appalachians in great numbers. Some helped their husbands establish homesteads in the Midwest, while others made the cross-country trek to Oregon and California. Over the years, many of the frontier settlements grew into sizable towns and cities. By the 1850s, white women were shopping, teaching school, and going to church on land that had been Indian territory just a few decades earlier.

During the same years, many enslaved black women were marched from their homes in the older regions of the South to new territories beyond the Appalachians, where they and the male slaves who accompanied them were set to work turning the area into the country's preeminent region for growing cotton and sugar. Here, as in the areas along the Atlantic coast, black and white women shared the stratified world of plantation life—a world that brought together some of the most privileged and most oppressed people in America living in close proximity yet separated by profound barriers of race and class.

Adding territory was not the only kind of national expansion going on during these years; the United States was also adding people. Between 1800 and 1865, the population increased from barely 4 million to about 35 million, thanks to a rising standard of living, which enabled people to live longer and have larger families. Immigration also increased dramatically; by 1865, about 250,000 people were entering the United States every year, 25 times as many as in the early 1820s. Irish immigrants predominated through much of this period, especially during the 10 years after 1845, when the great potato famine sent more than a million destitute Irish to American shores. Germans—mainly peasants and skilled craftsmen—formed the second-largest group of immigrants; by the late 1850s, they were arriving in even greater numbers than the Irish.

The growth of population fed the growth of towns and cities, and these offered distinctive opportunities for women. For poor women, like the Irish immigrants, there was the communality of a crowded ethnic neighborhood, as well as plenty of chances to augment the family income by working as a domestic servant or factory operative, sewing at home, or taking in lodgers. As for more prosperous urban women, most lived their lives in obedience to the emerging "cult of domesticity," which gave almost sacred significance to their role as homemakers. Nevertheless, the availability of poorer women to do the actual labor of housekeeping left many middle- and upper-class matrons free to spend at least some of their time on other activities. Thousands threw themselves into the era's many reform associations, working for such causes as temperance, child welfare, prison reform, improving conditions for female workers, and abolishing slavery. In 1848 they also organized the nation's first convention for women's rights—a landmark event that set an agenda for generations to come. Women's roles expanded further during the Civil War, when, in addition to filling in for their absent husbands, both northern and southern women played an important part in providing supplies for their respective armies and arranging for the soldiers' medical care.

The principal reason that so many working-class women could find jobs during the years between 1800 and 1865—and that so many middle-class wives could afford to stay out of the job market—was that as the country expanded in size and population, its economy was expanding as well. Despite a few serious financial panics, the wealth generated in the many good years substantially increased the number of husbands who earned enough to support their wives as ladies of leisure. Women of this class had two significant roles in the economy: They bought food, clothes, and furnishings for themselves and their families, and they employed domestic servants. Meanwhile, for the working-class women who did not wish to be maids, the expanding economy produced thousands of new factory jobs—a type of employment that generally involved long hours and relatively low pay, but which many women found preferable to domestic service.

Overall, as the United States expanded in territory, population, and wealth between 1800 and 1865, the opportunities available to women also expanded, though they were hardly transformed. Most white women continued to manage their houses and care for their husbands and children; most Indian women continued the difficult task of holding their families together as they moved further and further west; and most black women concentrated on maintaining the difficult balance between their obligations to their white masters and their efforts to see to the needs of their families. Nevertheless, there were some signs of change. Women constituted most of the country's first generation of factory workers. They also helped shape the course of antebellum social reform; they began to articulate an agenda for extending their own social, political, and economic rights; and during the Civil War they assumed unprecedented levels of responsibility, both in military hospitals and on the home front. Finally, with the end of the Civil War came the most dramatic change of all: the abolition of slavery, a change so far-reaching for both black and white women that its full implications would not be clear for many years to come.

With only one man in this pioneer family group, we can be sure that the women shared in the heavy labor along the trail, besides doing their housekeeping tasks.

White Women Move West

Year by year during the early nineteenth century the settled area expanded westward, pushed both by immigrant families and by young native-born couples seeking greater opportunities along the frontier. For both groups, the availability of cheap land out west and the soaring demand for American wheat and corn in Europe (as well as in America's own growing cities) offered the promise of better times in the new territory.

Most of the white women who moved west between the Revolutionary and Civil wars settled with their families in the region between the Appalachian Mountains and the Mississippi River. At first, the pioneers generally established themselves along the two great navigable rivers, the Ohio and the Mississippi, but as canals and railroads spread out across the land, the settlers spread out as well.

By 1850, towns beyond the Appalachians were growing larger, and Cincinnati, St. Louis, and Chicago each had a population of more than 100,000. Nevertheless, most western women lived on farms, carrying out the same duties that had shaped their grandmothers' lives: cooking, washing, sewing, cleaning, child care, carrying water, keeping the garden, and milking the cows. In addition, most of these women endured the

Overland trails

— Oregon Trail, 1834–58

— California Trail, 1841–59

— Santa Fe Trail, 1800–80

— state border, 1880

physical strain of frequent childbirth. Rural women's lives did change in some ways during the early 1800s, however: Farm families in this era were more likely to raise cash crops for distant markets and were more likely to buy products such as cloth and nails that their grandparents' generation had had to make themselves. In addition, as settlement increased, there was more chance for social contact. Nevertheless, many western women went weeks and sometimes months without any companionship beyond their own families.

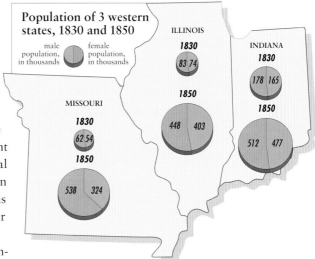

Population of 3 western states, 1830 and 1850

Starting in the 1840s, some women ventured even further west, traveling the overland trails to the Pacific coast. Most of these women (who constituted about one out of every seven pioneers on the trail) journeyed with their families in large wagon trains. It was an arduous trip, clouded by uncertainty, the fear of Indians (though attacks were relatively few), and the knowledge that the party must reach the coast before the autumn snows began. On the trail, women packed and unpacked the wagons, cared for the cows that traveled with them, saw to the children, carried water, cooked over the campfire, patched and repatched their families' clothes, and did what they could for the sick and the dying.

Originally, most pioneers headed to Oregon, but by 1850 the United States had won possession of California (as well as Texas and New Mexico) in the Mexican War, and gold had been found at Sutter's Fort. After that, California drew the most settlers. The Mexican population there was rapidly dispossessed of its land, and by the outbreak of the Civil War, Americans had dominated California's growing farm communities and mining towns. In this territory, the preponderance of men ensured that any woman willing to cook, sew, and do laundry for bachelors would find a flock of eager customers, and that any unmarried woman could have her choice of husbands.

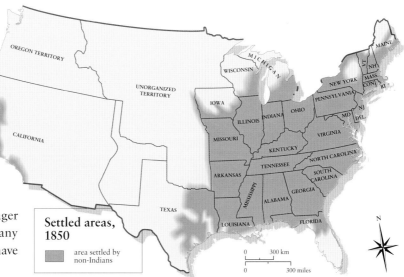

Settled areas, 1850

area settled by non-Indians

The Uprooting of Native American Women

The expansion of white women across the American continent during the early nineteenth century could not have occurred without the dispossession of the Indian women and their families who had lived there for centuries. This dispossession had a long history. Before the arrival of Columbus, the Indian population of North America was at least 4 million and may have been as high as 18 million. Yet by 1600 it numbered less than 1 million, and by 1750 it had fallen to 600,000.

The Europeans could not control their diseases, which wreaked havoc in Native American society, but they could control their weapons, and these they also used against the Indians. The early settlers in both Virginia and New England engaged in battles that wiped out whole tribes of neighboring Indians. From then on, as European settlement pushed westward, the Indians retreated before them. Some of the moves were precipitated by battles; others were negotiated by treaty—or rather, by a succession of treaties, each one breaking earlier promises so as to push the Indians further west. The accompanying map, showing the many Indian villages in the Great Lakes region during the late 1700s, suggests what was lost as Indian families were forced to leave the lands they had inhabited for generations. Moreover, as they retreated, they were often driven into the territory of other tribes, precipitating further conflict and migration.

By the 1830s, the last sections east of the Mississippi that had been set aside for Indians were surrounded on all sides by hungry white settlers. Evicted once more by the federal government, the Creeks of Alabama, the Cherokees of

Indian territory in the Great Lakes region, 1768

▲   Indian village

⌂   British fort

♜   fort

●   white settlement

▨   zone contested between tribes

═══   modern borders

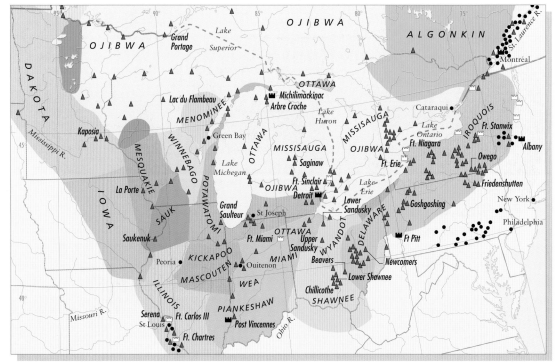

Georgia, and the Chicasaws and Choctaws of Mississippi were all forced to accept territory west of the Mississippi that was considered unfit for white settlement. The Cherokees' painful journey on foot to their new home on the inhospitable plains is known as the Trail of Tears. Tribes that resisted, like the Sauks in Wisconsin Territory, the Fox in Iowa Territory, and the Seminoles in Florida, were also forced to move into new areas west of the river. When white women organized a national petition drive to protest the brutal resettlement process, the effort helped them develop skills they would use more successfully in the abolition movement, but it had little impact on Indian removal. By the 1840s there were almost no Indian territories left east of the Mississippi.

Through all this sorry history, Indian women struggled to maintain their families, care for their children, and fulfill their roles in tribal society. Yet one can imagine how difficult this must have been, living as they did with the constant threat of war; the experience of seeing one's children, one's friends, and perhaps one's whole village wiped out by disease; the forced moves into unfamiliar territory; the conviction that each move would be followed by another one; and growing doubts about the future of the very institutions that held Native American society together: the clan, the tribe, and their connection to the land.

Driven from their ancestral lands in 1838, thousands of Cherokees walked the 800-mile "Trail of Tears" to Indian Territory in Oklahoma; one-quarter died on the way.

Indian land cessions, 1784–1859

	land ceded by 1783
	land ceded 1784–1809
	land ceded 1810–19
	land ceded 1820–29
	land ceded 1830–39
	land ceded 1840–49
	land ceded 1850–59
	Indian land, 1859

Urban Women before the Civil War

America's cities expanded more rapidly between 1800 and 1860 than at any other time in the nation's history. Fed by new immigration, the expansion of railroads and canals, and the rise of manufacturing, 10 cities passed the 100,000 mark by 1860, while the population of New York City soared to 800,000. By the time of the Civil War, about one American woman in five lived in a community larger than 2,500.

For the millions of urban wives who did not work outside their homes, the antebellum years introduced a revolutionary new role: the middle-class lady of leisure. Before 1800, nearly all urban married women except the very wealthy devoted much of their time to producing household goods, such as clothes, fabric, and food. Some of these goods were consumed by the family, while others were sold, but in either case, producing them represented economically significant work. Urban wives also participated in the economy by assisting their husbands in their home-based shops or stores.

Several factors combined to change this situation during the early nineteenth century. First, the expansion of commerce and the growth of manufacturing diminished the significance of home production and, therefore, of the housewife herself as a home producer. Second, as urban areas grew more densely populated, many families moved to new residential neighborhoods, leaving the husbands' businesses behind in the commercial district. This separation of work and residence significantly curtailed wives' participation in their husbands' occupational lives.

These changes help explain why women of the antebellum era were less *able* to contribute to their families' income, but another change, occurring at the same time, made women's contribution less *necessary*. As the American econ-

Rochester neighborhoods, New York, 1827, 1834

- central business district
- middle-class residential block
- working-class residential block
- mixed residential block

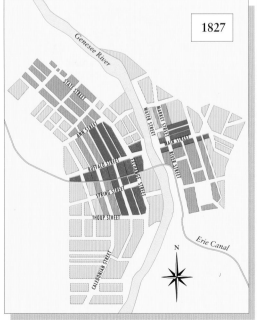

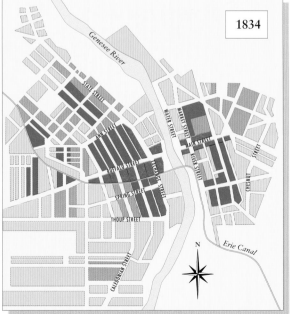

omy expanded during the early nineteenth century, the country developed an increasingly prosperous middle class. By the antebellum years, millions of urban men were earning enough as merchants or lawyers or even well-paid clerks to support their families without help from their wives. Meanwhile, a new wave of immigration—particularly from Germany and Ireland—filled American cities with young women willing to do domestic work for very low wages. Under these circumstances, it became a mark of status for the middle-class woman to withdraw from physical labor and concentrate on presiding over her "separate sphere"—the family home—making it a haven to which her husband could retreat from the harshness of the marketplace. Her servants, instead of working beside their mistress in the production of household goods, now devoted their primary efforts to maintaining her home according to the standards of bourgeois respectability.

In the eighteenth century, an urban housewife might have been singled out for praise because of her skill as a weaver or baker. The antebellum urban gentlewoman was more likely to be judged by the environment she created—the attractiveness of her appearance, the efficiency of her servants, the comfort of her parlor, the conviviality of her dinner table. Indeed, so compelling was this "cult of domesticity" that even women in extremely pinched circumstances strained their resources to meet the new standard of urban gentility.

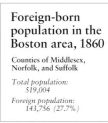

Foreign-born population in the Boston area, 1860

Counties of Middlesex, Norfolk, and Suffolk

Total population: 519,004

Foreign population: 143,756 *(27.7%)*

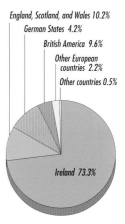

England, Scotland, and Wales 10.2%

German States 4.2%

British America 9.6%

Other European countries 2.2%

Other countries 0.5%

Ireland 73.3%

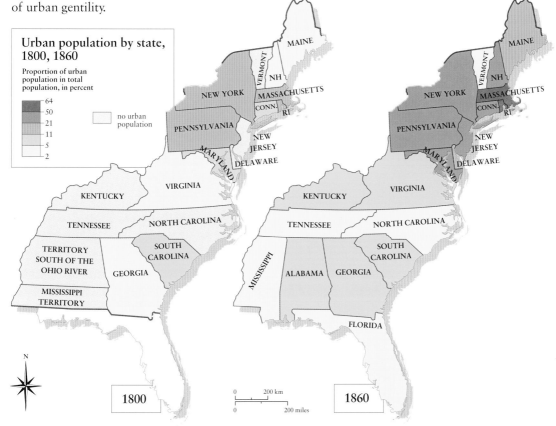

Urban population by state, 1800, 1860

Proportion of urban population in total population, in percent

- 64
- 50
- 21
- 11
- 5
- 2

no urban population

1800

1860

0   200 km

0   200 miles

N

Working Women of Antebellum America

This picture of a Massachusetts textile mill in the 1820s reflects two revolutionary innovations: the huge scale of the factory, and the workforce composed mainly of young women.

Look at a picture of women working in a Massachusetts textile mill in the 1820s and you see the first wave of America's industrial revolution. England's manufacturing cities were already famous for their ugliness and brutality, but many believed America could escape that fate by building "factories in the forest" that blended harmoniously with rural life. In fact, mill towns like Lowell, Massachusetts, grew quickly into cities; but during the early years of industrialization conditions in the New England factories were relatively benign. Instead of a permanent proletariat, the workers consisted mainly of farmers' daughters earning a few years' wages before they married. The factory regime was rigid but not unduly harsh, and many of the young women appear to have enjoyed their economic independence and the sociability of life in the big company-run boardinghouses.

Even as Lowell's fame spread, however, the conditions that had made it famous were changing. Financial pressures, particularly after the Panic of 1837, led the owners to drive down their labor costs in any way they could. Wages were cut, hours lengthened, machines speeded up, and operatives were required to oversee a growing number of machines. In response, some of the young women grew less docile. Proclaiming their rights as workers and as "daughters of freemen," they staged walkouts, organized unions, and helped lead statewide protests for a 10-hour day. The activists rarely managed to generate mass support, however, and they were relentlessly opposed by the factory owners, who took the women's unfeminine militance as justification for driving them harder. Conditions worsened steadily, and by the 1850s the number of Yankee farm girls in the Lowell mills had dropped sharply, while the proportion of Irish immigrants rose from 7 to 50 percent.

Women with any choice in the matter gravitated to other occupations, particularly the growing field of teaching. But those with fewer alternatives continued to do factory work, laboring not only in textile mills but also in book binderies, shoe factories, garment mills, and printing plants. In these workplaces, female operatives were nearly always paid less than men, and their choice of jobs was more limited. Moreover, their male coworkers tended to see them as a threat. Even though helping women earn equal wages would have protected the men from having their own wages undercut, it was much more common for men to protest, and sometimes strike, so as to keep women out of the workplace.

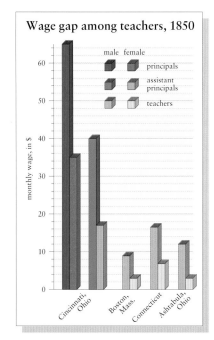

Wage gap among teachers, 1850

male female

principals

assistant principals

teachers

monthly wage, in $

Cincinnati, Ohio

Boston, Mass.

Connecticut

Ashtabula, Ohio

Women who had to work after marriage often did sewing at home; the pay was low and the volume heavy, but it did permit them to keep an eye on their children while they labored. Meanwhile, domestic service accounted—as it always had—for the largest amount of female employment. Irish immigrant women, in particular, crowded into the eastern cities, where they competed for work in private households. These domestic servants formed an uneasy relationship with their middle-class mistresses, highlighting by their very presence the fact that in order for one group of women to pursue the cult of domesticity, another group must spend their lives working for wages.

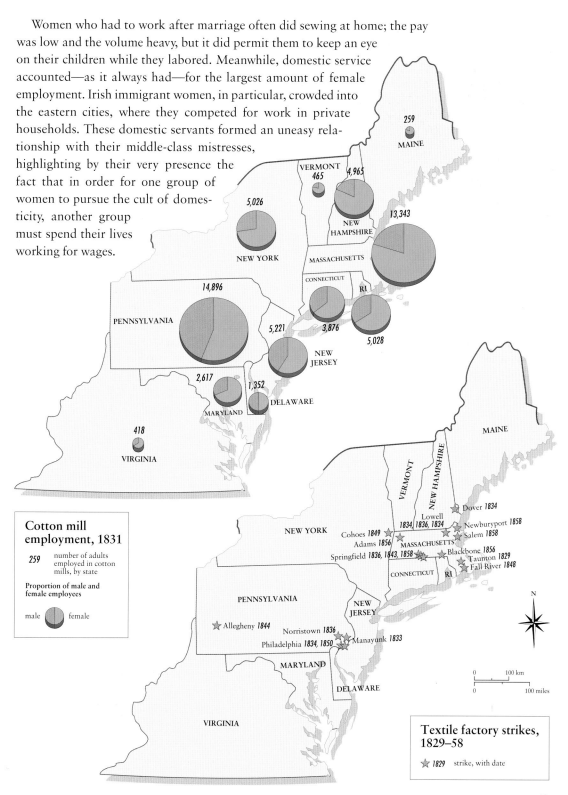

Cotton mill employment, 1831

259   number of adults employed in cotton mills, by state

Proportion of male and female employees

male   female

Textile factory strikes, 1829–58

⭐ 1829   strike, with date

41

Black and White Women on the Plantation

By the late 1850s, the 15 slave states of the South stretched from Maryland to Texas. The Mexican War and the expulsion of the Indians had opened huge new tracts for settlement, just when cotton was emerging as America's most valuable export. Thousands of white planters moved into the new territory, bringing their families and slaves with them. Even planters in the Upper South benefited from the boom by selling their extra slaves to the expanding cotton kingdom.

Enslaved women had always had to struggle to sustain their family ties. Their marriages had no legal standing, they had limited control over the lives of their children, and they were vulnerable to rape by masters and overseers. Now the changing patterns of southern agriculture brought further dislocation and hardship. Women forced to move west with their masters faced separation from their loved ones, a grueling march of several hundred miles, and the hard labor of carving out a plantation in virgin territory. Even those who remained along the eastern coast were often affected by the expanding slave trade, which deprived many mothers of their children and separated about 300,000 couples between 1820 and 1850.

Wherever they lived, most female slaves were agricultural laborers, rising before sunrise and working in the fields beside the men until dark. At night they returned to the slave quarters—a cluster of shacks built within sight of the overseer's house. The typical slave cabin, which might house one or several families, had a dirt floor, little furniture, a few corn-husk mattresses, and some pots and pans. Slaves received one or two outfits of clothes and a pair of shoes each year, as well as weekly rations of rice, peas, molasses, meat, and tobacco. Female slaves were treated better in the United States than elsewhere, but the effect of their inadequate diets, hard labor, drafty housing, and poor medical care can be seen in the fact that their infant mortality rate was more than double that of whites.

The white mistress had a very different experience of plantation life. Even on the south-western frontier, the "big house" was always the best-built struc-ture on the prop-erty, and some of these houses were among the most luxurious

1 main house
2 garçonnières (young men's dormitories)
3 plantation offices
4 dovecote
5 stable
6 carriage house
7 foreman's house
8 slave hospital
9 slave quarters
10 sugar mill
11 sugar house
12 blacksmith shop
13 scale house
14 barn and stable

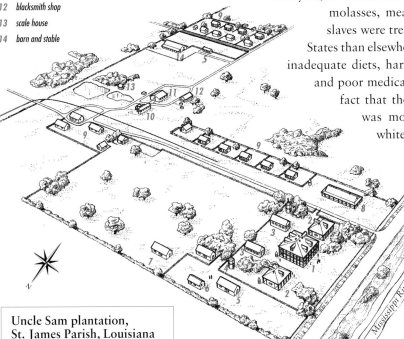

Uncle Sam plantation,
St. James Parish, Louisiana

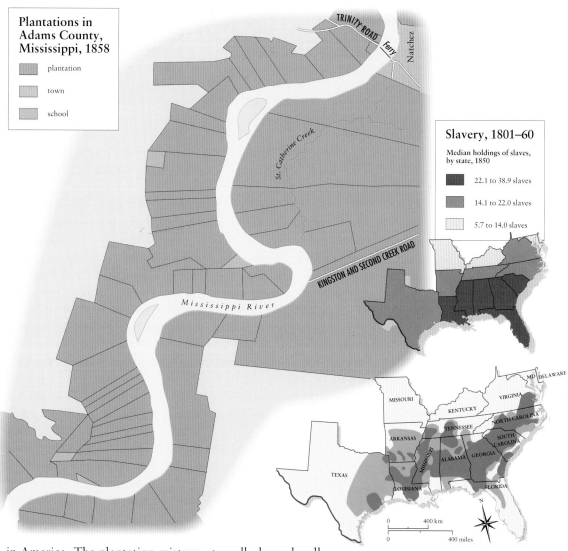

Plantations in Adams County, Mississippi, 1858

- plantation
- town
- school

TRINITY ROAD

Ferry

Natchez

St. Catherine Creek

KINGSTON AND SECOND CREEK ROAD

Mississippi River

Slavery, 1801–60

Median holdings of slaves, by state, 1850

- 22.1 to 38.9 slaves
- 14.1 to 22.0 slaves
- 5.7 to 14.0 slaves

MD | DELAWARE

MISSOURI

KENTUCKY

VIRGINIA

TENNESSEE

NORTH CAROLINA

ARKANSAS

SOUTH CAROLINA

ALABAMA | GEORGIA

MISSISSIPPI

TEXAS

LOUISIANA

FLORIDA

0   400 km

0   400 miles

in America. The plantation mistress ate well, dressed well, and rarely did physical labor. Yet she had far less leisure than her middle-class counterpart in northern cities. Besides being expected to act as a deferential wife, gracious hostess, and nurturing mother, she had heavy supervisory duties, presiding over the whole system of cooking, baking, sewing, gardening, fruit culture, poultry raising, dairying, food preservation, and informal medical care that sustained plantation life.

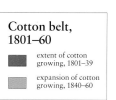

Cotton belt, 1801–60

- extent of cotton growing, 1801–39
- expansion of cotton growing, 1840–60

Within the big house, the mistress and her female slaves moved through a complicated daily ballet, sharing the same space, both subordinate to the white master, yet separated by race and status. The tensions of their relationship must have grown sharper still whenever a mulatto child appeared, reminding both mistress and slave of the dark and complicated patterns that connected their lives.

Women and Antebellum Reform

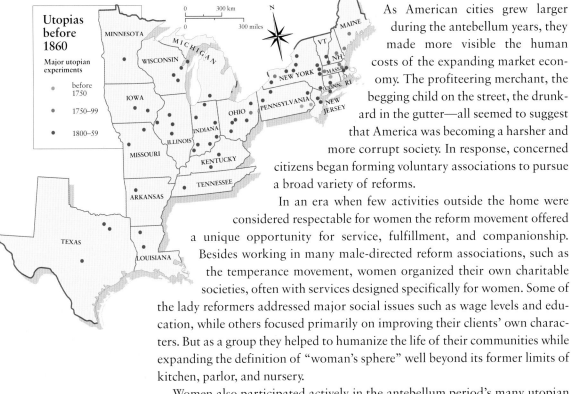

Utopias before 1860

Major utopian experiments

- before 1750
- 1750–99
- 1800–59

0   300 km
0   300 miles

MINNESOTA

MICHIGAN

WISCONSIN

MAINE

VT

NH

NEW YORK

MASS.

CONN. RI

IOWA

PENNSYLVANIA

NEW JERSEY

OHIO

INDIANA

ILLINOIS

MISSOURI

KENTUCKY

TENNESSEE

ARKANSAS

TEXAS

LOUISIANA

As American cities grew larger during the antebellum years, they made more visible the human costs of the expanding market economy. The profiteering merchant, the begging child on the street, the drunkard in the gutter—all seemed to suggest that America was becoming a harsher and more corrupt society. In response, concerned citizens began forming voluntary associations to pursue a broad variety of reforms.

In an era when few activities outside the home were considered respectable for women the reform movement offered a unique opportunity for service, fulfillment, and companionship. Besides working in many male-directed reform associations, such as the temperance movement, women organized their own charitable societies, often with services designed specifically for women. Some of the lady reformers addressed major social issues such as wage levels and education, while others focused primarily on improving their clients' own characters. But as a group they helped to humanize the life of their communities while expanding the definition of "woman's sphere" well beyond its former limits of kitchen, parlor, and nursery.

Women also participated actively in the antebellum period's many utopian communities, which pressed the drive for social reform further by experimenting with entirely new systems of property and family relations. Few of these settlements (except the Oneida community) challenged the division of labor between the genders, but their communal living patterns gave women a very different daily experience from the typical nuclear household of the period. And women's lives were of course profoundly affected by unconventional family arrangements such as the Shakers' celibacy, the Mormons' polygamy, and the Oneida community's group marriage.

Women's commitment to reform changed antebellum society, but it also changed their own lives. As they participated more actively in community life, they became increasingly conscious of their own capacity and of their legal and social constraints. Why should they be expected to defer to men in so many fields of life? Why should married women be denied the right to hold, buy, or sell property, sue or be sued, enter into contracts, or keep their own wages? A growing sense of the injustices they faced set the stage for the first women's rights meeting, held at Seneca Falls, New York, in 1848. (One of its conveners was Lucretia Mott, a dedicated abolitionist who had been denied admission to an international antislavery congress because of her sex.) Although the participants' "Declaration of Sentiments," modeled on the Declaration of Independence, went far beyond what could be achieved at the time, it laid out an agenda that would inspire women for generations thereafter.

1   Guntersville, AL   1820   Catherine Brown, daughter of Indian chief, opens Christian school for Indian girls.

2   Washington, DC   1820   Ann Marie Becroft organizes city's first seminary for black girls.

3   Boston, MA   1820   Women organize Society for Employing the Poor.

4   Troy, NY   1821   Emma Willard founds the nation's first endowed women's school, Troy Female Seminary; pioneering curriculum.

5   Philadelphia, PA   1821   Two hundred working-class black women form mutual-aid association, Daughters of Africa Society.

6   Hartford, CT   1823   Catherine Beecher and sister organize Hartford Female Seminary; promotes women's education and teacher training.

7   New York, NY   1823   Women organize New York Asylum for Lying-In Women to help poor pregnant women.

8   Philadelphia, PA   1823   Mary Waln Wistar organizes Female Prison Association of Friends, visits women prisoners.

9   Florissant, MO   1825   Sisters of the Sacred Heart found Female Indian Seminary.

10   New York, NY   1827   Black women organize African Dorcas Society, meet weekly to sew clothes for children.

11   Baltimore, MD   1829   First black female religious order in Catholic church opens orphanages and schools for black children and emancipated slaves.

12   New York, NY   1829   Frances Wright lectures to mixed audiences: attacks religion, wealth, marriage, promotes universal education.

13   Canterbury, CT   1832   Prudence Crandall, Quaker, accepts black student at her girls' school. Arrested, house attacked by mob.

14   Boston, MA   1832   Maria Stewart, first American-born female lecturer, speaks on black women's rights and abolition.

15   Cincinnati, OH   1832   Catherine Beecher establishes Western Female Institute, stressing teacher training.

16   Boston, MA   1833   Sarah Hale starts Boston Seaman's Aid Society to give work to poor widows.

17   New York, NY   1834   New York women form Female Moral Reform Society to fight prostitution and help prostitutes.

18   New York, NY   1836   Ernestine Potowski Rose organizes first petition (six signatures) to state legislature regarding married women's property rights.

19   New York, NY   1836   Two white Quaker women start Colored Orphan Asylum, with mostly black female staff.

20   Brattleboro, VT   1836   Anna Hunt Marsh donates $10,000 to found one of first mental hospitals in U.S.

21   South Hadley, MA   1837   Mary Lyon founds Mount Holyoke, first American college only for women; women raise most of the funds needed.

22   Litchfield, CT   1839   Eight years before Seneca Falls, local women's group composes unsigned Declaration of Independence for Women.

23   Boston, MA   1843   Dorothea Dix reports to state legislature on the inhumane treatment of the mentally ill in Massachusetts prisons.

24   Baltimore, MD   1844   Quakers set up Women Friends Association for Visiting the Penitentiary; help female prisoners.

25   Providence, RI   1844   Paulina Wright Davis gives lectures on anatomy to women, using a Paris store dummy.

26   Trenton, NJ   1845   Dorothea Dix presents a devastating report on New Jersey poorhouses; leads to the state's first mental hospital.

27   New York, NY   1846   Women open what is possibly the world's first halfway house for released female prisoners.

28   St. Paul, KS   1847   Four Sisters of Loreto found mission and school for Osage Indian girls.

29   Gardner, MA   1847   Lucy Stone gives her first feminist lecture from her brother's pulpit in the Congregation Church.

30   Seneca Falls, NY   1847   Amelia Bloomer publishes The Lily, first paper for women owned and operated by a woman.

31   Senecca Falls, NY   1848   First women's rights convention in the United States.

Selected reform activities by women, 1820–48

Angelina Grimké, Abolitionist

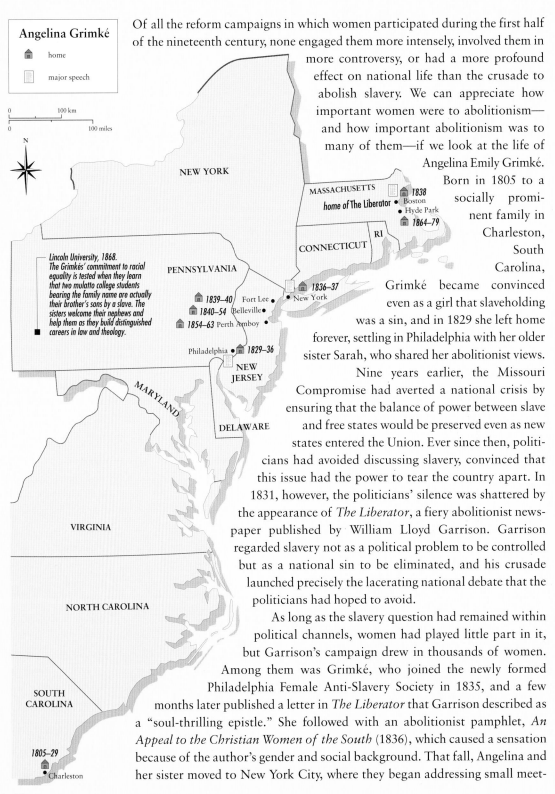

Angelina Grimké

🏠 home

▥ major speech

0 ——— 100 km
0 ——— 100 miles

N

NEW YORK

MASSACHUSETTS
home of The Liberator ● Boston
● Hyde Park
🏠 *1838*
🏠 *1864–79*

RI

CONNECTICUT

Lincoln University, 1868.
The Grimkés' commitment to racial
equality is tested when they learn
that two mulatto college students
bearing the family name are actually
their brother's sons by a slave. The
sisters welcome their nephews and
help them as they build distinguished
careers in law and theology.

PENNSYLVANIA

🏠 *1836–37*
New York

🏠 *1839–40* Fort Lee ●
🏠 *1840–54* Belleville ●
🏠 *1854–63* Perth Amboy ●

Philadelphia ● 🏠 *1829–36*

NEW
JERSEY

MARYLAND

DELAWARE

VIRGINIA

NORTH CAROLINA

SOUTH
CAROLINA

1805–29
🏠
Charleston

Of all the reform campaigns in which women participated during the first half of the nineteenth century, none engaged them more intensely, involved them in more controversy, or had a more profound effect on national life than the crusade to abolish slavery. We can appreciate how important women were to abolitionism— and how important abolitionism was to many of them—if we look at the life of Angelina Emily Grimké. Born in 1805 to a socially promi- nent family in Charleston, South Carolina, Grimké became convinced even as a girl that slaveholding was a sin, and in 1829 she left home forever, settling in Philadelphia with her older sister Sarah, who shared her abolitionist views.

Nine years earlier, the Missouri Compromise had averted a national crisis by ensuring that the balance of power between slave and free states would be preserved even as new states entered the Union. Ever since then, politi- cians had avoided discussing slavery, convinced that this issue had the power to tear the country apart. In 1831, however, the politicians' silence was shattered by the appearance of *The Liberator*, a fiery abolitionist news- paper published by William Lloyd Garrison. Garrison regarded slavery not as a political problem to be controlled but as a national sin to be eliminated, and his crusade launched precisely the lacerating national debate that the politicians had hoped to avoid.

As long as the slavery question had remained within political channels, women had played little part in it, but Garrison's campaign drew in thousands of women. Among them was Grimké, who joined the newly formed Philadelphia Female Anti-Slavery Society in 1835, and a few months later published a letter in *The Liberator* that Garrison described as a "soul-thrilling epistle." She followed with an abolitionist pamphlet, *An Appeal to the Christian Women of the South* (1836), which caused a sensation because of the author's gender and social background. That fall, Angelina and her sister moved to New York City, where they began addressing small meet-

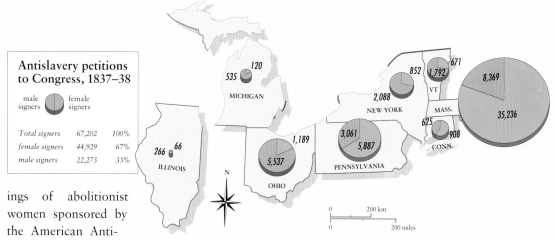

Antislavery petitions to Congress, 1837–38

male signers / female signers

Total signers	67,202	100%
female signers	44,929	67%
male signers	22,273	33%

MICHIGAN — 535, 120

ILLINOIS — 266, 66

OHIO — 5,537, 1,189

PENNSYLVANIA — 3,061, 5,887

NEW YORK — 852, 2,088, 35,236, 8,369

VT — 1,792, 671

MASS. — 625, 908

CONN.

N

0 — 200 km

0 — 200 miles

ings of abolitionist women sponsored by the American Anti-Slavery Society. Both Grimkés were elected officers of the society in 1837, and that same year Angelina published another pamphlet: *An Appeal to the Women of the Nominally Free States*. The Grimké sisters' unique background, reinforced by Angelina's special power as an orator, began attracting men as well as women to their lectures, and they soon undertook a five-month tour of New England, addressing 40,000 people in 67 towns. When critics called their public advocacy unfeminine, each sister published a strongly worded pamphlet defending women's right to speak out on any subject.

The Grimkés' 1837 lecture tour coincided with an abolitionist campaign to flood Congress with antislavery petitions. So many petitions were submitted that the House of Representatives passed a "gag rule" prohibiting their presentation—a response that only caused the abolitionists to redouble their efforts, and reinforced their assertion that slavery was corrupting the fundamental processes of American democracy. The Grimkés promoted the petition campaign in their lectures, and in 1838, when Angelina became the first woman ever to address a committee of the Massachusetts legislature, she presented a petition that contained 20,000 signatures.

The pinnacle of Angelina's speaking career came a few months later, at an antislavery convention in Philadelphia, where her passionate hour-long address held the audience spellbound while a hostile mob raged outside. Garrison said that "as the tumult from without increased . . . her eloquence kindled, her eyes flashed, and her cheeks glowed."

Just two days before the convention, Grimké had married a leading abolitionist, Theodore Dwight Weld. Soon after the wedding, the Welds and Sarah moved to Fort Lee, New Jersey, and retired from public life, although they did write a compilation of reports from southern newspapers called *American Slavery as It Is: Testimony of a Thousand Witnesses* (1839)—upon which Harriet Beecher Stowe drew extensively for her novel, *Uncle Tom's Cabin*.

Angelina's public career had lasted only four years, and the movement to which she had devoted herself soon divided into factions. Nevertheless, by contributing so wholeheartedly to the evangelical abolitionism of the 1830s, she and her sister had participated in a crucial chapter in the nation's history, one which forced all Americans to confront the gravest problem in their society.

"I stand before you as a southerner, exiled from the land of my birth, by the sound of the lash, and the piteous cry of the slave. I stand before you as a repentant slaveholder. I stand before you as a moral being . . . and as a moral being I feel that I owe it to the suffering slave, and to the deluded master, to my country and the world, to do all I can to overturn a system of complicated crimes, built upon the broken hearts and prostrate bodies of my countrymen in chains, and cemented by the blood and sweat and tears of my sisters in bond."

from a speech by Angelina Grimké to a committee of the Massachusetts House of Representatives, Feb. 21, 1838.

Southern Women during the Civil War

The Civil War (1861–1865) disrupted the lives of women in the South more than in the North because most of the fighting took place on southern soil and because such a large share of the southern male population entered military service. When we look at maps of southern battlefields and of the Union Army's march through Georgia, we need to think what this war sweeping across the South meant for the women and children in its path.

Plantation mistresses had always taken considerable responsibility for the "big house" and its outbuildings, but with most of the men gone to fight, they found themselves struggling to manage the entire agricultural operation on which their lives depended, using slaves who often showed little inclination to follow their orders. Living on land that could be bleakly isolated today and a battleground tomorrow, concerned about their menfolk at the front, uneasy with their slaves, and recognizing (perhaps for the first time) the heavy labor that had always been involved in sustaining their way of life, plantation mistresses struggled to learn and to master a role they had never expected to fill.

Slave women who remained on the plantations carried the brunt of the physical work left behind by the men. Many formerly privileged house slaves found themselves laboring in the fields, while even women accustomed to agricultural work strained to do the heavier jobs that men had performed in the past. Large numbers of male slaves had been taken away to work for the military, while those left behind often escaped as soon as the Union

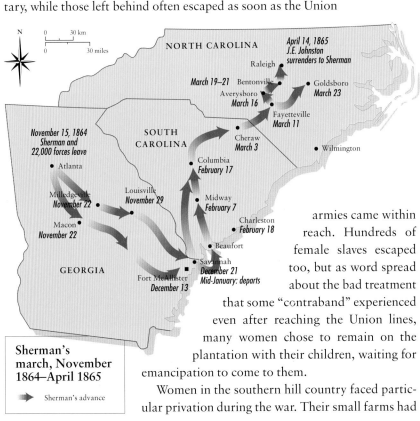

Sherman's march, November 1864–April 1865

→ Sherman's advance

armies came within reach. Hundreds of female slaves escaped too, but as word spread about the bad treatment that some "contraband" experienced even after reaching the Union lines, many women chose to remain on the plantation with their children, waiting for emancipation to come to them.

Women in the southern hill country faced particular privation during the war. Their small farms had

MISSOURI

WEST VIRGINIA

MARYLAND

DELAWARE

VIRGINIA

KENTUCKY

TENNESSEE

NORTH CAROLINA

ARKANSAS

SOUTH CAROLINA

MISSISSIPPI

ALABAMA

GEORGIA

LOUISIANA

FLORIDA

N

0   50 km

0   50 miles

Battles of the Civil War, 1861–65

Confederate state

slave state in the Union

★ Union victory

★ Confederate victory

☆ inconclusive

never provided more than a meager living, even with the unending toil of husbands and wives together. During the war the women strained every muscle to run their farms on their own. So desperate did conditions become in the hills that several state and local governments began distributing food to the needy women and their children. The distribution was not well organized, however, and most families survived (or failed to survive) on their own.

Women served the Confederacy in many ways besides filling in for their absent husbands. Thousands sewed for the soldiers, some did nursing, and some joined the army disguised as men. Others, like Belle Boyd, used their charm to beguile secrets from Union officers. Hill-country wives proved the least dedicated Confederates. They had never been particularly enthusiastic about secession, and as they watched their husbands carry a disproportionate share of the fighting in what they perceived as a war to protect the rich planters, they moved from skepticism to outspoken criticism. By the final years of the war, many women in the hill country were actively encouraging their husbands to desert.

Northern Women during the Civil War

While most southern women of both races shared the common experience of managing without men in a war-torn agricultural society, northern women's wartime experience was more varied.

In rural areas, women pitched in to keep farms and plantations running, just as they did in the South. However, northern women had the advantage of operating within a thriving economy, and only in the border states did they face the additional terrors of marauding soldiers and nearby battles. The approach of emancipation was also less dramatic in the few slave states of the North because slavery was less prevalent there, and free blacks were already a familiar part of society.

About one northern man in five did military service, but since draftees could avoid enlistment by paying a large fee or hiring a substitute, poor men (including Irish immigrants) did more than their share of the fighting. They expressed their resentment in uprisings such as the three-day draft riot in New York City in 1863—a riot in which women participated so violently that several hundred of them were arrested. When, despite such resistance, hundreds of thousands of working-class men marched off to war, their families were often left in desperate straits. Struggling to survive on their own, some wives scraped by on low-paid factory work, while others turned to domestic service.

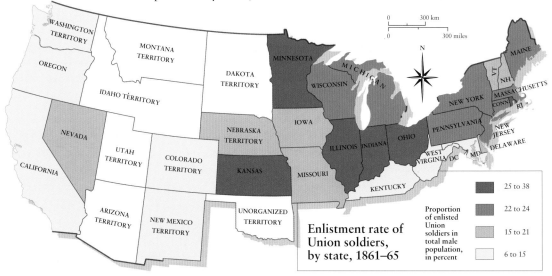

Enlistment rate of Union soldiers, by state, 1861–65

Proportion of enlisted Union soldiers in total male population, in percent

- 25 to 38
- 22 to 24
- 15 to 21
- 6 to 15

For northern women of the leisure classes, the Civil War represented something quite different: an opportunity to participate in the most compelling national effort since the abolition movement. One group of women collected 400,000 signatures on petitions urging Congress to pass a constitutional amendment ending slavery. Others focused on organizing medical and relief services for the Union Army. Soon after the war began, Elizabeth Blackwell, the nation's first female doctor, convened a meeting of 3,000 women in New York City. Out of that meeting and others grew the U.S. Sanitary Commission, which ultimately became the largest voluntary association in the country, with

Soldiers' wives, like this one photographed by Matthew Brady in 1862, often traveled with their husbands, and many brought their children along as well.

7,000 branches throughout the North. Men generally held the leadership roles in "the Sanitary"—and in other similar organizations—but most of the tens of thousands of volunteer workers were women. Together they organized huge fund-raising "Sanitary Fairs" and bazaars; supplied army camps and hospitals with bandages, medicine, clothing, food, and volunteer nurses; provided food and lodging for soldiers on leave; and provided assistance to destitute wives and families of soldiers.

Women also made advances during the Civil War in the field of military nursing, which until then had generally been performed by poorly trained soldiers. Thanks to the efforts of the Sanitary's many volunteers, and of enterprising individuals like Clara Barton and the formidable "Mother" Bickerdyke, women proved themselves indispensable in this field, setting the stage for the emergence of nursing as a female profession during the decade after the war.

Black and white, rich and poor, northern and southern, American women accomplished things during the Civil War that they had never done before. The next challenge would be to consider how these newfound capacities could be applied in postwar society.

NEW YORK
Albany
MASS.
Boston
Chicago
CONN.
Providence
New York
RI
Cleveland
PENNSYLVANIA
Brooklyn
ILLINOIS
INDIANA
OHIO
Pittsburgh
Philadelphia
NEW JERSEY
Wheeling
MARYLAND
DEL.
Cincinnati
Washington
WEST VIRGINIA
Louisville
Cairo
KENTUCKY

N

Activities of the U.S. Sanitary Commission

●   sanitary fairs held, 1863–64

■   main depot for the Commission

0   100 km

0   100 miles

PART III: SEEKING A VOICE: 1865–1914

During the years between the end of the Civil War in 1865 and the outbreak of World War I in Europe in 1914, American women in many different walks of life sought to increase the opportunities available to their sex and to make their voices heard more clearly in the dialogue of national life. Not all women chose to follow this path, and not all who tried succeeded, but enough ground was gained so that by 1914 they had managed to broaden substantially the general perception of what American women could or should do with their lives.

In the workplace, women made their presence felt most significantly simply by their increasing numbers. By 1900, more than 5 million American women (about 20 percent of all women) were working for pay. Most women's wages were low, and many worked in private households, which gave them little opportunity to combine forces or articulate their grievances. But in some work locations the growing concentration of women created new possibilities for collective action. In the urban garment shops and textile mills of the Northeast, for instance, female workers launched a series of protests that drew national attention. Many of the strikers were new immigrants, and their cultural diversity made their ability to work together all the more impressive. Few gained all their demands, but their periodic victories revealed the potential on which future organizing efforts could be built.

Women were also breaking new ground in the world of white-collar occupations. Already by 1900, most of the country's secretaries, teachers, librarians, and nurses were women; if few of these jobs promised wealth or significant advancement, they provided more autonomy than domestic service and pleasanter conditions than factory work. Women found it much more difficult to enter higher-status fields such as law and medicine, but during the years between 1865 and 1914 a determined group of female pioneers took the difficult first steps—persuading professional schools to admit them, fighting for the right to take the necessary licensure exams, then building their careers despite receiving little help from the networks that supported their male colleagues.

Work as such was nothing new to American women, of course. Throughout the country's history, white and Indian women had contributed their unpaid labor to maintaining their families, while most black women had toiled as slaves. But the generation of employed females who came of age toward the end of the nineteenth century gained new independence because so many worked away from the control of their families and earned their own money. Furthermore, although most women stopped working after a few years to get married, a significant number in the professions and the arts chose to remain single, making their homes alone or with female friends and devoting their lives to their careers. Overall, from the militant striker to the indispensable secretary to the strongminded lady doctor, the efforts of working women during these years opened a range of new possibilities for those who followed.

Meanwhile, other women were making their mark in the field of social reform. At this time, unprecedented levels of immigration were overwhelming American cities, while the growing hostility between capital and labor seemed to be straining the very fabric of society. In response, a new generation of female reformers—many of them recent college graduates—dedicated their lives to improving social conditions and bridging the gulf between the classes. As part of that dedication, many of them made the same choice as the female lawyers and doctors described above: They remained unmarried.

These single women formed the backbone of the emerging settlement house movement and the new U.S. Children's Bureau, and they gave continuity and direction to a vast array of other reform organizations addressing issues such as housing, factory safety, child labor, mother's pensions, juvenile justice, women's unions, woman suffrage, and public health. Their efforts were in turn reinforced by the hard work and financial contributions of millions of other women who combined voluntarism with marriage. Married women broadened the base of the reform movement, infusing social clubs, temperance societies, church groups, farm women's clubs, and civic associations all across the country with a new activist orientation. By serving not only as loyal soldiers but as leaders in so many social battles, the female reformers of the Progressive Era demonstrated yet another way in which women could make their voices heard.

Even though work in a sweatshop meant low pay and poor conditions, it offered young women considerably more sociability and free time than domestic service.

Black women's clubs were an important part of this movement, but their exclusion from the white women's club network reminds us that even fighters for social justice often wore blinders when it came to racial equality. This fact becomes all the more striking when we remember that during this same period—a veritable highwater mark of American social reform—an elaborate structure of legal segregation was being erected in the South, virtually all black voters were being disenfranchised, and the former slaves' dream of economic independence was giving way to the sharecropping system. Few white female reformers had much to say on these topics, nor did most of them comment on the ongoing destruction of Indian tribal life in the West or on the rejection experienced by Indians who tried to join white society. The growing difficulties faced by so many black and Indian women is a potent reminder that the Progressive Era was in many respects painfully unprogressive.

Even the many women who did benefit from the changes occurring during these years were sharply aware of the ground yet to be gained. Most who worked were still poorly paid in relation to either what men earned or what it cost to live. Female professionals were still fighting for recognition, only 11 of the 48 states had granted women full suffrage, and the double standard of morality continued to make sexual dalliance a minor transgression for a man but a potential source of lifetime disgrace for a woman. Yet if the years between 1865 and 1914 left many aspirations still unrealized, they nevertheless opened more possibilities than ever before for women to speak out and be heard in American society.

Women in the South during Reconstruction

During the first decade after the Civil War, black and white women strove to take up their lives again in a South transformed by war and Emancipation. Many white women had assumed their troubles would end when the men came home from the war. But by 1865 one out of every four Confederate soldiers was dead, transportation networks were wrecked, southern cotton no longer dominated the world market, and thousands of farms and plantations had been left with no seed, no machinery, and no livestock. Moreover, the federal program of Reconstruction put the entire South under the military control of the victorious northern Republicans in Congress. Besides the army, there was the federal Freedmen's Bureau, which opened offices and schools for the ex-slaves throughout the South—just one more proof that the old world was gone forever.

In the hill country, these years brought a steady erosion of the subsistence agriculture that had sustained generations of yeomen farmers. Compelled to buy machinery and fertilizer in order to compete in the postwar agricultural market, thousands of families lost their farms and ended as tenants, forced to grow the only crop their creditors would support: cotton. As farm families struggled to pay for food they used to grow themselves, malnutrition became a pervasive presence in the hills.

In the former slave counties, white planters hoped to return to the gang labor practiced during slavery, but few had the cash to pay wages. The ex-slaves, for their part, could not obtain what they wanted—their own farms—because they had been given no land and were prevented by whites from buying any. Ultimately, whites and blacks compromised on a third system: sharecropping. Using the one commodity they had in abundance—land—the planters divided their plantations into small plots, which they rented to tenant farmers, providing each with a house, seed, and tools in exchange for a share of the crop.

The ex-slaves found sharecropping at least preferable to wage labor, and freedom did fulfill some of their other aspirations. Black males could vote, and though black women (like all women) could not, they attended rallies and parades, and spoke up in public meetings. In addition, they eagerly attended the Freedmen's Bureau schools. Most important, emancipation gave them a chance to reconstruct their families. Freed couples thronged public offices to legalize their marriages, while others walked hundreds of miles to find family members scattered by the slave trade.

As part of this family-building effort, many black women hoped to stop doing field labor. The ideal of the provider husband and homemaker wife had wide appeal; in addition, many freedwomen associated field work with the memory of sexual abuse by

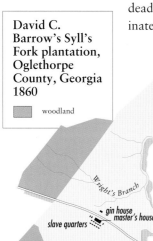

David C. Barrow's Syll's Fork plantation, Oglethorpe County, Georgia 1860

◾ woodland

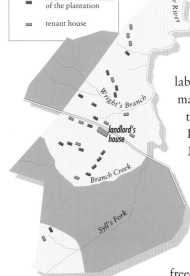

1881

▬ house of former slave of the plantation

▭ tenant house

white overseers. White planters, on the other hand, wanted as large a labor force as was possible, and the new Republican regime, though more sympathetic to the ex-slaves, was intent on reviving southern agriculture. Gradually, legal and economic pressure forced black women to return to the fields. Reconstruction had not brought the millennium yet laboring for and with one's family under the sharecropping system was still preferable to the coercion of slavery.

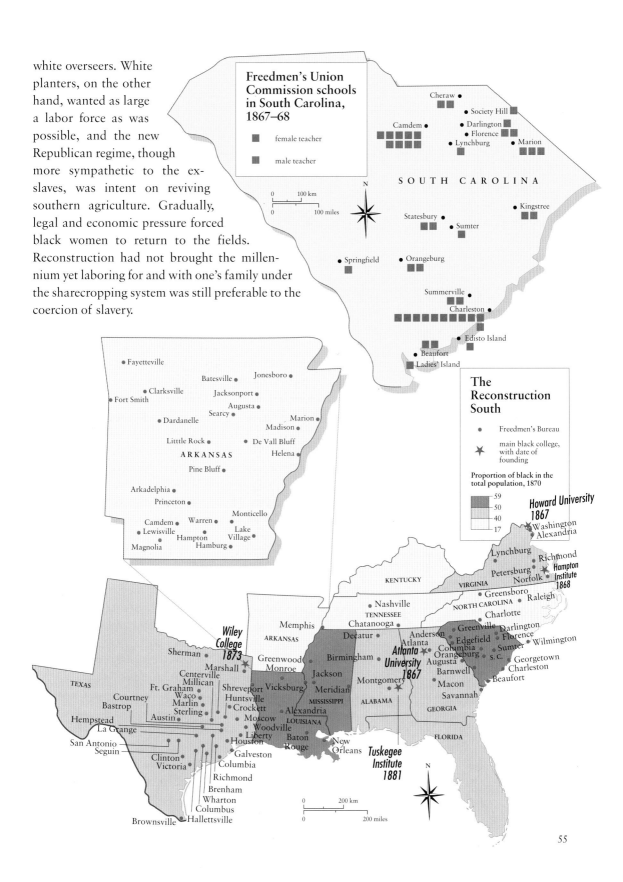

Freedmen's Union Commission schools in South Carolina, 1867–68

■ female teacher

■ male teacher

0   100 km
0   100 miles

N

SOUTH CAROLINA

Cheraw
Society Hill
Camdem
Darlington
Florence
Lynchburg
Marion
Kingstree
Statesbury
Sumter
Springfield
Orangeburg
Summerville
Charleston
Edisto Island
Beaufort
Ladies' Island

Fayetteville
Batesville
Jonesboro
Clarksville
Jacksonport
Fort Smith
Augusta
Searcy
Dardanelle
Marion
Madison
Litttle Rock
De Vall Bluff
Helena
ARKANSAS
Pine Bluff
Arkadelphia
Princeton
Monticello
Camdem
Warren
Lewisville
Lake Village
Hampton
Magnolia
Hamburg

The Reconstruction South

● Freedmen's Bureau

★ main black college, with date of founding

Proportion of black in the total population, 1870

59
50
40
17

Howard University 1867
Washington
Alexandria

Lynchburg
Richmond
Petersburg
Norfolk
Hampton Institute 1868
VIRGINIA
Greensboro
Raleigh
NORTH CAROLINA
Nashville
Chatanooga
TENNESSEE
Charlotte
ARKANSAS
Memphis
Decatur
Anderson
Greenville
Darlington
Atlanta
Edgefield
Florence
Wiley College 1873
Greenwood
Birmingham
Atlanta University 1867
Columbia
Orangeburg
Wilmington
Sherman
Monroe
Jackson
Augusta
Sumter
Georgetown
Marshall
Meridian
Montgomery
Barnwell
S.C.
Charleston
Centerville
Millican
Shreveport
Vicksburg
MISSISSIPPI
Macon
Beaufort
Ft. Graham
Waco
Huntsville
ALABAMA
Savannah
Courtney
Marlin
Crockett
GEORGIA
Bastrop
Sterling
Moscow
TEXAS
Austin
Woodville
Hempstead
Liberty
La Grange
Houston
Baton Rouge
San Antonio
Galveston
New Orleans
FLORIDA
Seguin
Columbia
Tuskegee Institute 1881
Clinton
Richmond
Victoria
Brenham
Wharton
Columbus
Brownsville
Hallettsville
LOUISIANA
Alexandria

KENTUCKY

N

0   200 km
0   200 miles

Women of Color Face New Adversity

Spending per child in public schools, by state, 1890 and 1910

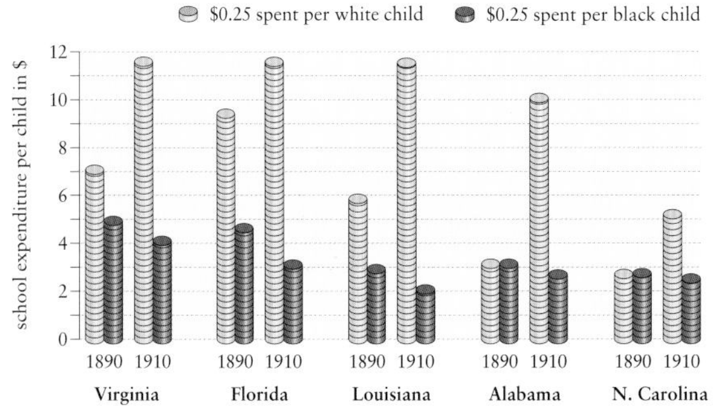
$0.25 spent per white child
$0.25 spent per black child
school expenditure per child in $
0
2
4
6
8
10
12
1890 1910
Virginia
Florida
Louisiana
Alabama
N. Carolina

Neither African-American nor Native American women could have been considered privileged in the late 1860s. But by 1900, the position of both groups had worsened dramatically.

For African Americans, Reconstruction had represented at least halting progress toward racial equality. By 1876, however, Reconstruction was dead, a victim of southern whites' hostility and northern whites' indifference. The ex-slaves' hope of economic equality would go unfulfilled for generations to come. One indication can be seen in the accompanying map of a southern tobacco plantation in 1910; there, 50 years after emancipation, black sharecroppers were still living in the former slave quarters. Across the South, each black woman working in the fields provided yet another reminder of the distance between the ex-slaves' dream of yeoman respectability and their actual place in the postwar economy.

The end of Reconstruction also ended African Americans' hope for civil equality, as southern states began passing laws requiring segregation in virtually every public space where white and black paths might cross. Racial separation had always been the custom, but the new system expanded the practice and backed it up with mob violence. The final step in subordinating African Americans was disenfranchisement. Between 1890 and 1905, every southern state enacted new laws preventing black males from using their new right of suffrage. This process disempowered black women as well, since it silenced the voters most committed to their interests and virtually ended the political life of the black community, in which women had often participated.

While southern black women were experiencing these losses, Native American women were watching their entire way of life disappear. As white settlers pushed westward, the Indians who lived in their path were forced to move again and again. Meanwhile, the buffalo herds on which they lived were wiped out by expanding farms, the railroad, eastern sportsmen, and the U.S. Army.

From the 1870s on, the Indians were forced onto reservations, where they were

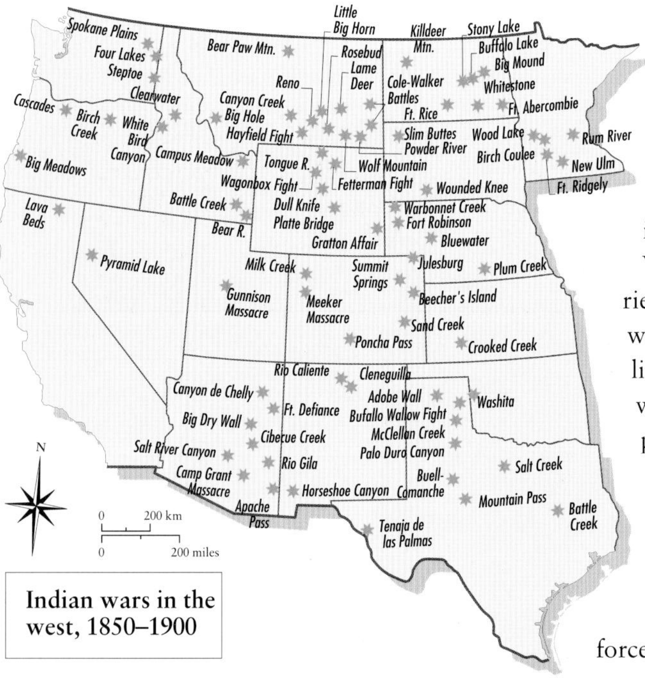
Spokane Plains
Four Lakes
Steptoe
Clearwater
Cascades
Birch Creek
White Bird Canyon
Big Meadows
Lava Beds
Bear Paw Mtn.
Canyon Creek
Big Hole
Hayfield Fight
Campus Meadow
Reno
Little Big Horn
Rosebud
Lame Deer
Cole-Walker Battles
Ft. Rice
Killdeer Mtn.
Stony Lake
Buffalo Lake
Big Mound
Whitestone
Ft. Abercombie
Slim Buttes
Powder River
Wood Lake
Birch Coulee
Rum River
New Ulm
Ft. Ridgely
Tongue R.
Wolf Mountain
Wagonbox Fight
Fetterman Fight
Wounded Knee
Battle Creek
Dull Knife
Warbonnet Creek
Fort Robinson
Bear R.
Platte Bridge
Gratton Affair
Bluewater
Pyramid Lake
Milk Creek
Summit Springs
Julesburg
Plum Creek
Gunnison Massacre
Meeker Massacre
Beecher's Island
Sand Creek
Poncha Pass
Crooked Creek
Rio Caliente
Cleneguilla
Canyon de Chelly
Adobe Wall
Washita
Big Dry Wall
Ft. Defiance
Bufallo Wallow Fight
Cibecue Creek
McClellan Creek
Salt River Canyon
Palo Duro Canyon
Rio Gila
Salt Creek
Camp Grant Massacre
Buell-Comanche
Horseshoe Canyon
Mountain Pass
Apache Pass
Tenaja de las Palmas
Battle Creek
N
0 200 km
0 200 miles

Indian wars in the west, 1850–1900

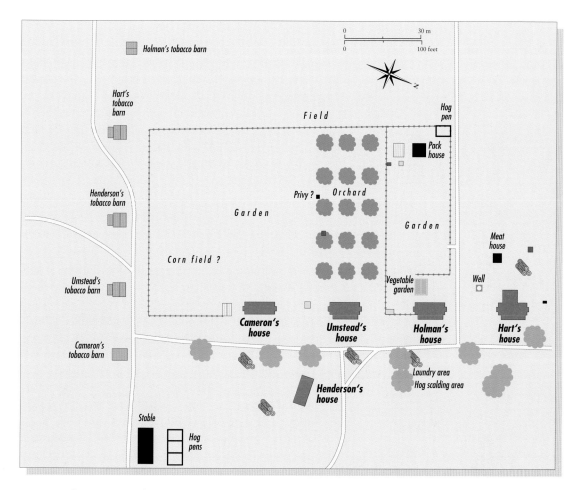

Tenant farmer accommodations in former slave quarters, Horton's Grove plantation, North Carolina, about 1910

■	residence
▦	tobacco barn
▥	ordering house
■	hen house
□	corn crib
⊶⊷⊶	fence
🪵	wood pile

aggressively encouraged to accept "civilized" customs like nuclear households and private property. Even sympathetic reform groups like the mainly white Women's National Indian Association supported this policy. The WNIA particularly stressed the need for Indian men to become better providers, so that their wives would no longer have to raise crops and make tools and clothes. Yet in urging this reform, the WNIA paid little heed to the economic status that Indian women had achieved by carrying out important roles in the tribal economy.

Women in tribes that resisted the federal reservation policy endured years of battle, flight, privation, and final defeat. The U.S. Army was no respecter of age or gender, and hundreds of women and children were killed by federal soldiers during the so-called Indian Wars. Yet tribes who acquiesced fared hardly better. Their land allotments were too small to support them, and even these meager holdings were continually eroded by speculators' trickery. As for the myth of assimilation, thousands of Indian mothers suffered the pain of having their children taken away to government boarding schools, only to see them return years later, rebuffed by white society yet having lost all sense of connection with the world of their parents.

Settling the Prairies

Between 1860 and 1900, the number of American farms rose from 2 million to nearly 6 million. Most of the new ones were established on the Great Plains—the vast treeless region between the Mississippi River and the Rocky Mountains that had been left to the Indians long after both coasts were settled. Now it was the only frontier remaining, and once the Indians were expelled from there too, hundreds of thousands of pioneer families moved out onto the plains.

Most families spent their first prairie year in a sod-block house or dugout. Both types of dwellings attracted an army of flies, beetles, and fleas, and both turned muddy every time it rained. Even the wooden houses that came next offered minimal protection against the ceaseless wind, winter blizzards, extreme summer heat, frequent droughts, and periodic hordes of locusts. Meanwhile, long-term deflation and international competition caused farm prices to drop steadily. Many families lost their farms, and those who kept them had to work desperately to hold their own.

Women's experience on the prairie was particularly grueling. Equipped only with what they had been able to bring with them, they learned to do without commodities that even the poorest eastern women took for granted, such as matches, kerosene, soap, coffee, and window glass. Clothes had to be made out of old blankets and tents, and gardens raised in the searing prairie wind.

One source of excitement and companionship for women during these years was the Farmers' Alliance, a reform movement that swept the South and the Great Plains during the 1880s. Working through an extensive network of local chapters, the alliance held huge camp meetings at which female as well as male lecturers held farm families spellbound

An eastern town: Poughkeepsie, New York, 1899

1 square mile section

- main built-up area
- loosely built-up area
- railroad
- church
- school or college
- theater or hall
- hotel
- hospital
- bank
- factory
- other important building

A prairie township: West Blanchard, North Dakota, 1892

1 square mile section

- 6 original land division
- subdivision
- cluster of farm buildings

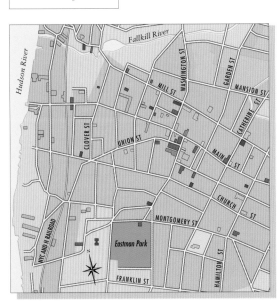

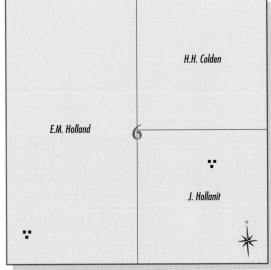

with their gospel of agrarian solidarity and revitalized democracy. Theory came with a heavy dose of advocacy, as when the famed alliance speaker Mary Ellen Lease advised the gathered farmers to "raise less corn and more hell." As the alliance evolved into a political party (the Populists), women played a smaller role since they could not vote, yet they remained a lively presence within the movement, helping to articulate a reform agenda that would resurface repeatedly in the decades ahead.

Prairie women's lives grew somewhat easier by 1900, thanks to the expansion of the railroad and the invention of the mail-order catalogue (starting with Montgomery Ward in 1872), which opened a world of inexpensive goods to farm families across the plains. The isolation of prairie life—something that women felt with particular acuteness—also lessened somewhat as more people arrived in the territory. Nevertheless, the large acreage of even modest farms in this dry country meant that homesteads remained a considerable distance apart, and prairie women often went weeks without seeing anyone but their husbands and children. The accompanying maps illuminate the isolation of that life, contrasting the North Dakota farmhouse alone on the prairie with the dense pattern of shops, schools, churches, and houses in a typical eastern town.

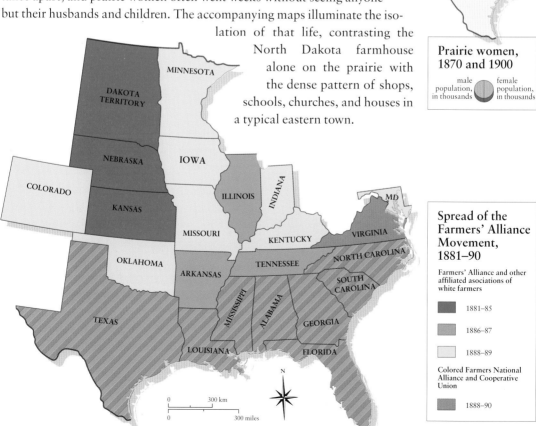

Prairie women, 1870 and 1900

male population, in thousands / female population, in thousands

Spread of the Farmers' Alliance Movement, 1881–90

Farmers' Alliance and other affiliated asociations of white farmers

1881–85

1886–87

1888–89

Colored Farmers National Alliance and Cooperative Union

1888–90

The Lady of the House

The idea that women should inhabit a "separate sphere" centered on home and family continued to prevail throughout the nineteenth and early twentieth centuries, shaping the lives of most middle- and upper-class women and defining a tantalizing ideal for those who needed to work for wages.

The late teenage years represented a crucial period during which a young woman must find a man whom she could trust to love and support her for the rest of her life. (The wrong choice could be disastrous, since divorce was both difficult and repugnant.) To win the right man, a young woman had to be attractive but not flashy, responsive but not too eager, virtuous but not dull, amusing but not competitive. Only by following these dictates, it was understood, could she get to play the roles for which she had been trained: wife and mother.

After courtship and marriage came domesticity. By the late nineteenth century an increasing number of middle- and upper-class wives pursued that calling in the suburban communities that had begun to develop around American cities. The suburban home seemed to embody the very essence of the domestic ideal. Commuting husbands could restore themselves in this haven every night, while their wives and children—who spent most of their time there—could preserve their purity and idealism uncontaminated by the industrial city that made their way of life possible.

The first suburbs, built along the train lines, accommodated only those who could afford the expense of commuting by rail. After 1890, however, the expansion of trolley and subway lines spurred the development of suburban housing that even clerks and skilled workmen could afford. By 1914, most cities were ringed with suburbs, ranging from modest communities near the downtown

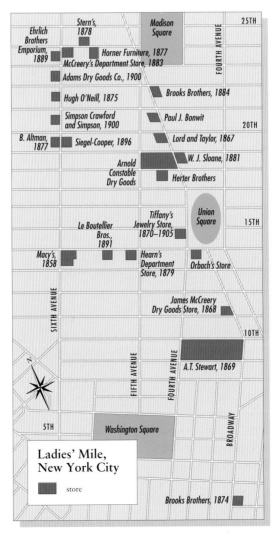

Ladies' Mile,
New York City
store

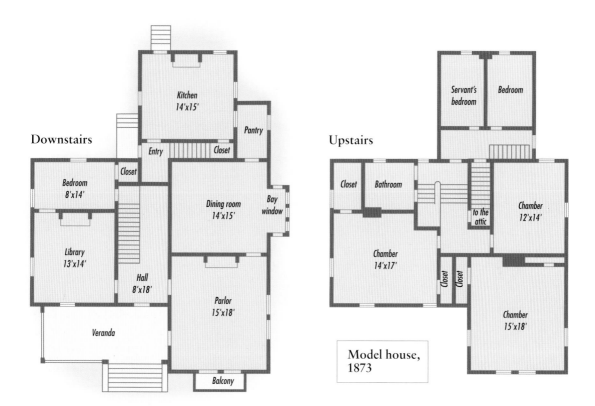

Downstairs

Kitchen
14'x15'

Pantry

Entry

Closet

Closet

Bedroom
8'x14'

Dining room
14'x15'

Bay
window

Library
13'x14'

Hall
8'x18'

Parlor
15'x18'

Veranda

Balcony

Upstairs

Servant's
bedroom

Bedroom

Closet

Bathroom

to the
attic

Chamber
12'x14'

Chamber
14'x17'

Closet

Closet

Chamber
15'x18'

Model house,
1873

center to comfortable middle-class neighborhoods further out, to elegant mansions in the more distant towns along the railroad. Yet all these communities shared certain elements: single-family houses, convenience to the city, and a daytime population consisting primarily of women, children, and the people who served them. Thus, even while the real estate market sorted suburban women out by class, the fundamental pattern of their lives reflected their common adherence to the doctrine of "woman's sphere."

Being a proper wife—whether urban, suburban, or rural—involved serious responsibilities for house and children, but it did not mean spending every hour at home, particularly for women who could afford household help. While men pursued their separate lives, many wives enjoyed a strong network of female associations. Sewing bees and church socials brought country women together. Prosperous urban and suburban matrons called on each other frequently, served together on charity boards, and spent hours in the handsome department stores and tearooms that had grown up to serve them in downtown districts like the famous Ladies Mile in New York City. Letter-writing also strengthened female bonds, often sustaining girlhood friendships for decades. The vitality of these female networks, combined with the sharp separation of activities by gender, may help to explain why during this period many women's closest emotional ties were to other women.

A New Wave of Immigrant Women

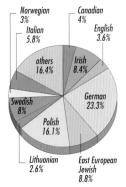

Chicago population, 1910

Origin of foreign-born

Norwegian 3%
Canadian 4%
Italian 5.8%
English 3.6%
others 16.4%
Irish 8.4%
Swedish 8%
German 23.3%
Polish 16.1%
Lithuanian 2.6%
East European Jewish 8.8%

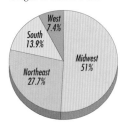

Origin of native-born

West 7.4%
South 13.9%
Midwest 51%
Northeast 27.7%

Between 1880 and 1920, more than 7 million women journeyed to the United States from other countries to establish new homes for themselves and their families. Many were wives or daughters traveling with their families; others were young mothers with children coming to join husbands who had arrived earlier. By 1905, total immigration averaged more than 1 million per year—far above previous levels and higher than any period thereafter until the 1990s. About one third of these newcomers were women.

Most earlier immigrants had come from Ireland, Germany, England, and Scandinavia, but during the 1890s the country began receiving huge numbers of Italians, Jews, Slovaks, Poles, Bohemians, Armenians, and Greeks. Expanding industrialization abroad was creating new jobs for northern Europeans, encouraging them to stay where they were, but it did little for the poverty-stricken millions living in eastern and southern Europe. Jews from that area had particular reason to emigrate, since, besides their poverty, they were subjected to continuing repression and periodic violence.

Eastern Europe did have some factories, and young women who had had a taste of industrial labor there hoped to find better pay and working conditions in America; some who had discovered left-wing politics also hoped for a chance to speak out more freely on political issues. The much larger number of women who had been housewives on farms or in Jewish shtetls had their own dreams: of a country where their husbands could earn enough to feed their families, where their sons would not be imprisoned or shot for political activism, where their daughters would not live in fear of Cossack raiders, and where their children might grow up to lead easier lives than they had led.

The new female immigrants soon discovered that for them life in America usually meant life in an industrial city. Among immigrant groups of the past, only the Irish had been so destitute that they had had to settle for urban wage

An arduous voyage behind her, a difficult transition ahead, this immigrant mother arrived with her children at Ellis Island in 1911.

work; most of the Germans, Scandinavians, and English had had enough savings to establish their own small businesses or farms. By contrast, the families who immigrated at the turn of the century were nearly as impoverished as the Irish had been, and by then there was little cheap land left in the West. Realizing that America's surging industrial growth represented their best opportunity, most of them settled in the country's growing cities.

Europeans were not the only newcomers converging on these cities. Others were country-bred Americans fleeing rural poverty and—in the case of southern blacks—the rising constraints and violence of racial segregation. Like the Europeans, these native-born migrants headed where the jobs were: the cities. Many welcomed the connections that were available in the dense urban neighborhoods, quite different from pioneering on the lonely prairie. But preferences aside, millions of men and women in this generation of migrants recognized that America's cities offered the best chance available to make a better life for themselves and their families.

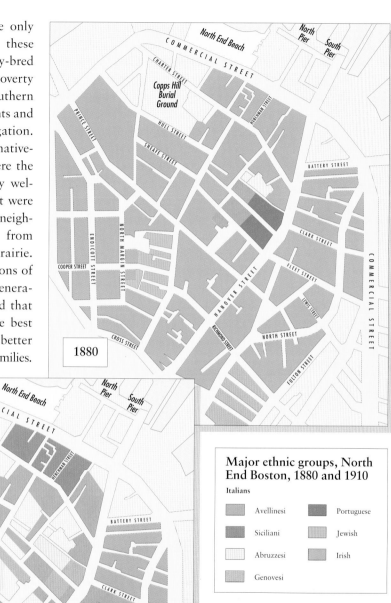

Major ethnic groups, North End Boston, 1880 and 1910

Italians

Avellinesi

Siciliani

Abruzzesi

Genovesi

Portuguese

Jewish

Irish

Making a Home in the Tenements

During the years between 1880 and 1920, millions of European-born women found themselves raising their families in the slums of American cities. The cheapest urban housing was usually to be found on the edge of industrial districts. Sometimes speculators threw up shoddy new buildings to house the immigrants; in other cases, older homes were subdivided. Public services—already strained by rapid urban growth—tended to be worst of all in the new immigrant neighborhoods. Garbage stood uncollected; sewage systems functioned erratically. Inside the tenements, there might—at best—be a sink and a toilet on each floor; more commonly, sanitary facilities were located in the basement or the backyard, so that all the water for cooking, cleaning, dishwashing, bathing, and laundry—as well as slops and chamber pots—had to be carried up and down several flights of stairs.

Apartments usually consisted of three or four rooms. In cities with row housing—such as New York and Baltimore—the inner bedrooms often had no windows or gave onto an airshaft so odorous that opening the window made things worse. In Philadelphia and Washington, D.C., poor people often lived on narrow courts and alleys squeezed in behind more prosperous homes. Even in cities where there was more space between buildings—such as Boston and San Francisco—the dirt and smells of the crowded streets and nearby factories seemed to permeate the houses, defeating every effort of mop or broom.

Extreme crowding made tenement housekeeping still more difficult. Stretching every penny, the newcomers typically lived in family groups of 10 or 12, with any extra space rented out to boarders. For the woman of the house, this arrangement increased the daily load of cooking, washing, and sewing, while further complicating the task of keeping clean and neat a space in which so many people led their lives.

Even settling for primitive housing in the least desirable districts and sleeping three and four to a room, most families found they could not survive on the men's earnings alone. Accordingly, for many women, the apartment also became a workshop where they might spend 10 or 12 hours a day doing handwork. The labor was draining and low-paid, but it permitted women to work at home, keeping an eye on their children while snatching scattered moments for housekeeping.

Tenement life was not all burdensome: Many immigrants remembered for years the warmth and sociability of the circle at the kitchen table. But for the women involved, the challenge of making a home in the tenements was a brutally hard responsibility.

Alley dwellings, Washington, D.C., 1912

As depicted in
The Monday Evening Club,
*Directory of Inhabited Alleys
of Washington, D.C.*

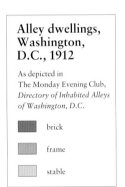

- brick
- frame
- stable

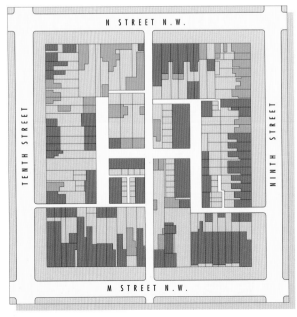

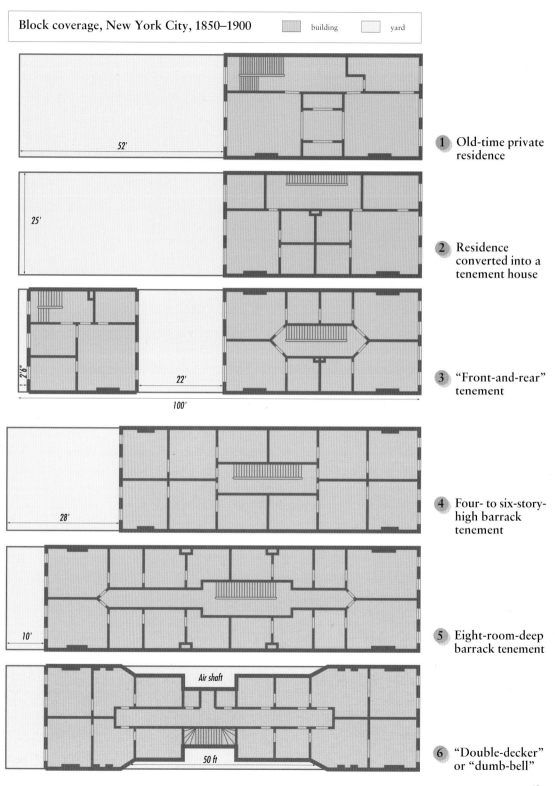

Block coverage, New York City, 1850–1900 ☐ building ☐ yard

1 Old-time private residence

52'

2 Residence converted into a tenement house

25'

3 "Front-and-rear" tenement

2'6" 22'

100'

4 Four- to six-story-high barrack tenement

28'

5 Eight-room-deep barrack tenement

10'

6 "Double-decker" or "dumb-bell"

Air shaft

50 ft

Working Women at the Turn of the Century

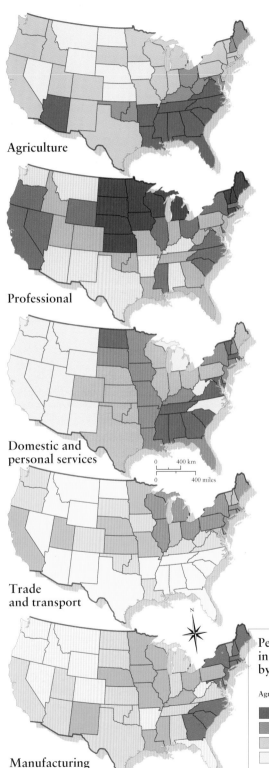

Agriculture

Professional

Domestic and
personal services

Trade
and transport

Manufacturing

0   400 km
0   400 miles

N

Women accounted for about one sixth of the American labor force in 1900 (compared with nearly one half in the 1990s). Overall in 1900, about one woman in five held a paying job. The clearest determinant of a woman's employment status was her marital status. Only 6 percent of married women were employed, compared to 44 percent of single women and 33 percent of widows and divorcées. This pattern reflected the strong cultural preference for wives to remain at home. In addition, the relatively high rate of employment among widows and divorcées reflected the financial vulnerability that women frequently experienced if they lost their husbands.

Nearly 40 percent of America's 5 million working women held service jobs, either in private households or in facilities such as hotels, restaurants, laundries, and hospitals. Service work was not viewed as particularly desirable because of its heavy physical demands, low pay, and long hours, yet in an era when many better-paying fields were closed to females, this kind of work did enable nearly 2 million women to support themselves or contribute to the income of their families.

Among service jobs, those in private homes were by far the most common, yet they were considered the least desirable. Many women perceived the work as demeaning and disliked the enforced closeness with their employers; ladies of the middle and upper class could be highly critical, not only of their servants' work performance but also of their dress, speech, and private lives. "Living in" enabled one to save money, but it exposed one to even closer scrutiny and

Percentage of women in total workforce by field and by state, 1900

all workers in a field
women workers
in this field

Agriculture	Professional	Domestic and personal services	Trade and transport	Manufacturing
8–29	39–50	43–57	11–20	20–29
4	32–38	36–42	9–10	16–18
3	30–31	29–35	6–8	12–15
2	22–29	14–28	3–5	4–11

sometimes to sexual harassment from the men of the household as well, so most domestics worked by the day if they could. Since women with any choice in the matter avoided domestic service altogether, jobs as household servants were held disproportionately by the two groups of women with the fewest options: African Americans (particularly in the South) and immigrants. African-American women provided a particularly large labor pool, because a far higher percentage of them continued to work after they married and because racial restrictions excluded them from nearly every nonservice occupation except agricultural labor.

Manufacturing work, which was the second-largest female occupational group (about 25 percent of the female workforce), is discussed in the following section. The rest of the female labor force was more or less equally divided between the category of "trade and transport" (which for women usually meant working as a secretary or sales clerk), and professional occupations, primarily teaching school. The pay earned by secretaries, sales clerks, and teachers was only slightly higher than what they might have earned in service or factory jobs, but the working conditions were better, the status higher, and the hours shorter. All three of these white-collar occupations were opening up increasingly to women; indeed, secretarial work was well on its way to becoming an exclusively female occupation. Yet the gender distinctions remained in the fact that women were paid significantly less than men for doing the same job and that supervisors were nearly always male.

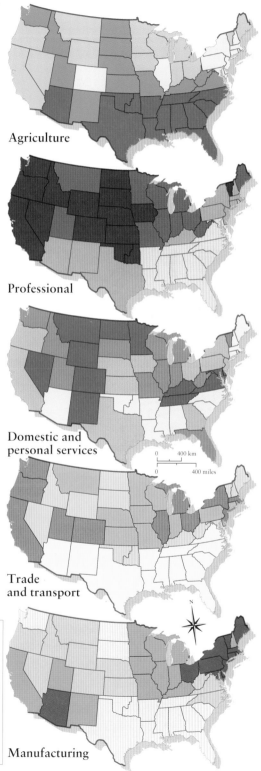

Agriculture

Professional

Domestic and
personal services

Trade
and transport

Manufacturing

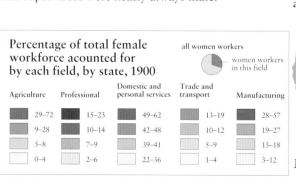

Percentage of total female workforce acounted for by each field, by state, 1900

all women workers
women workers in this field

	Agriculture	Professional	Domestic and personal services	Trade and transport	Manufacturing
	29–72	15–23	49–62	13–19	28–57
	9–28	10–14	42–48	10–12	19–27
	5–8	7–9	39–41	5–9	13–18
	0–4	2–6	22–36	1–4	3–12

Women in Factories

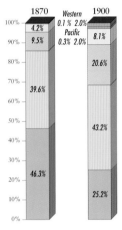

Women in manufacturing, by region, 1900

Share of the U.S. female manufacturing workforce (16 years and over) accounted for by each region

Women in manufacturing, by region, as proportion of female employees 16 years and over

By 1900 more than a million women were working in American factories. What had seemed a striking innovation in the textile mills of the 1820s had by the turn of the century become a familiar feature of the industrial scene. Some women tended huge mechanical looms in textile mills; others worked at sewing machines in crowded sweatshops or found jobs in shoe factories, cigar factories, or canneries. All faced the common hardships of industrial labor during this period: long hours, low pay, dirty and unsafe working conditions, and periodic spells of unemployment. This era did see the gradual establishment of laws limiting working hours for women, but enforcement was weak, and large segments of the female workforce remained unprotected.

Beyond these problems, female factory workers experienced certain further difficulties specifically because of their gender. Many male workers resisted the growing use of women in industry because they associated it with a process called "deskilling," in which complicated tasks were broken down into steps so simple that they could be done by the cheapest labor available: women and children. Deskilling had indeed made significant inroads, but most factories still maintained two gradations of work: one set of skilled jobs allocated to men and another set, at the lower end of the pay scale, assigned to women. In the garment trades, for instance, men did the cutting and pressing, while women performed simpler tasks such as sewing on pockets and buttons. In food processing, men did the baking while women were restricted to frosting and packaging. No amount of talent or industriousness could qualify a woman to be trained for a "man's job," and even women who had somehow acquired the skills were not allowed to practice them. Any employer who permitted a woman to cross this line risked a strike by his male employees.

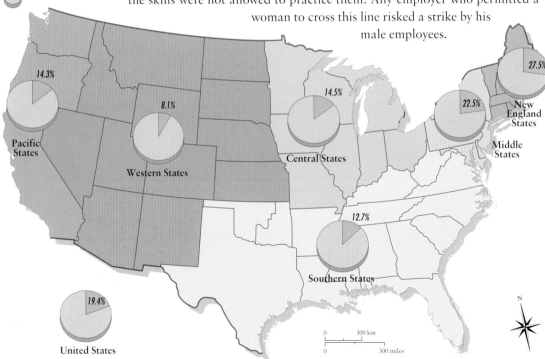

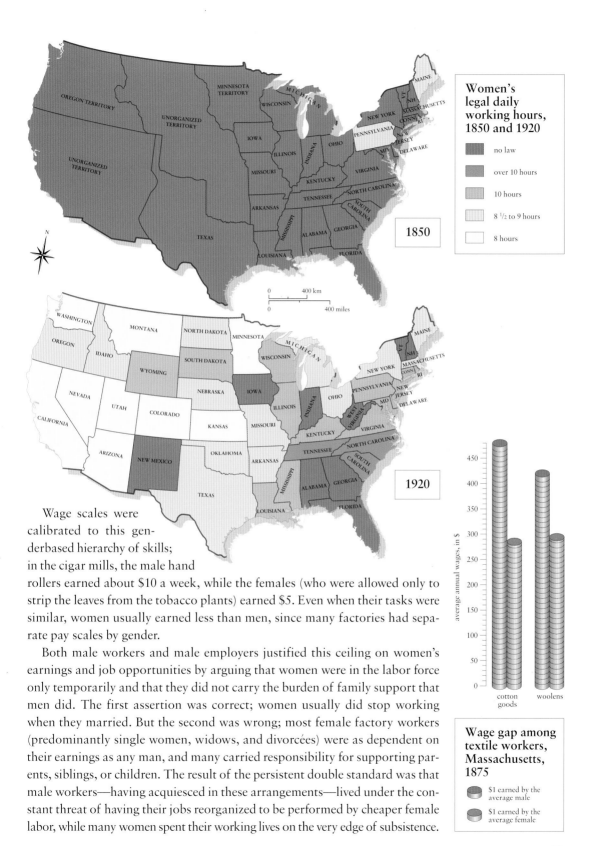

Women's legal daily working hours, 1850 and 1920

- no law
- over 10 hours
- 10 hours
- 8 ½ to 9 hours
- 8 hours

1850

0   400 km

0   400 miles

1920

average annual wages, in $

cotton goods

woolens

Wage gap among textile workers, Massachusetts, 1875

- $1 earned by the average male
- $1 earned by the average female

Wage scales were calibrated to this gen-derbased hierarchy of skills; in the cigar mills, the male hand rollers earned about $10 a week, while the females (who were allowed only to strip the leaves from the tobacco plants) earned $5. Even when their tasks were similar, women usually earned less than men, since many factories had separate pay scales by gender.

Both male workers and male employers justified this ceiling on women's earnings and job opportunities by arguing that women were in the labor force only temporarily and that they did not carry the burden of family support that men did. The first assertion was correct; women usually did stop working when they married. But the second was wrong; most female factory workers (predominantly single women, widows, and divorcées) were as dependent on their earnings as any man, and many carried responsibility for supporting parents, siblings, or children. The result of the persistent double standard was that male workers—having acquiesced in these arrangements—lived under the constant threat of having their jobs reorganized to be performed by cheaper female labor, while many women spent their working lives on the very edge of subsistence.

Women and the Unions

One major reason why women workers were unable to achieve better pay and job opportunities during the nineteenth and early twentieth centuries was the fact that they had no sustained and effective labor organization. Women did organize many unions from the 1830s on, but few of these unions survived more than a few years.

Besides the problems faced by all trade unionists women's unions faced some unique difficulties. First, many male unionists opposed the very idea of women in the workplace. Second, the female labor force was composed disproportionately of unskilled workers and immigrants, who were particularly difficult to organize. Third, many women thought of their work careers as only a brief interlude before marriage, so they were often reluctant to engage in the hard work necessary to build a union.

The first group to organize women on a major scale was the Knights of Labor, which came to national prominence during the early 1880s. At its peak, the Knights had an estimated 50,000 female members, of whom nearly one third were enrolled in assemblies that included both men and women. The Knights fell into decline in the late 1880s, however, and their successor, the American Federation of Labor, concentrated mainly on organizing skilled males.

The next wave of labor militance among female workers arose 20 years later in New York City's shirtwaist factories. Starting with scattered walkouts in 1908, the movement built to a massive strike in seversal cities in 1909–1910 that came to be called "the uprising of the 30,000." The strikers won many of their demands thanks, in part, to the Women's Trade Union League, which had been established a few years earlier to build connections among

Women's Assemblies of the Knights of Labor, by state, 1886

■ 1 assembly composed entirely of women

0   300 km

0   300 miles

N

upper-class female reformers, women workers, and the labor movement. The International Ladies Garment Workers Union acted more as follower than leader during this strike, but the society members of the WTUL proved stalwart allies, contributing most of the funds, faithfully walking the picket line, and drawing wide press coverage when they were subjected to the same police brutality as the strikers.

Over the next several years women engaged in numerous strikes across the country, some assisted by the WTUL and others backed by the radical Industrial Workers of the World. Among the latter was the 1912 uprising in the textile mills of Lawrence, Massachusetts. The Lawrence workers won their strike and, giving the lie to the idea that immigrant women could not be organized, celebrated their victory by singing the communist hymn, "The Internationale," together in a dozen different languages.

Even successful strikes during this period rarely brought union recognition. Furthermore, the dangerous conditions that caused the death of 146 young workers in the Triangle Shirtwaist fire—just a year after the victorious end of the strike in New York—bore eloquent testimony to the ground that still remained to be won by women workers and their unions.

Ethnicity of Chestnut Street

- native-born
- Canadian French
- Russian and Armenian
- German and Austrian
- English and Scottish
- French
- Italian, Greek, Turkish, and Syrian

Neighborhoods of "The Plains," Lawrence, Massachusetts, 1912

- textile mill
- house of female strike activist

Sister Carrie in the Industrial City

Carrie visits The Fair Store: "There was nothing there which she could not have used—nothing which she did not long to own. The dainty slippers and stockings, the delicately frilled skirts and petticoats, the laces, ribbons, haircombs, purses, all touched her with individual desire, and she felt keenly the fact that not any of these things were in the range of her purchase."

Theodore Dreiser,
Sister Carrie

Theodore Dreiser's great novel *Sister Carrie* begins in 1889, with an 18-year-old girl from Wisconsin riding the train to Chicago. Dreiser's heroine, Carrrie Meeber, was not the only one making this kind of trip. During the late nineteenth century, America's economic expansion was creating thousands of new jobs, mostly in the cities, and attracting thousands of young women from the countryside to fill them. A small proportion of the newcomers were qualified for professional careers; another small fraction would end up supporting themselves as prostitutes. But the majority would find work in factories, stores, offices, restaurants, and people's homes. This labor force represented something new on the urban scene: a large population of young single women earning their own wages and moving with considerable independence through the city.

Like many other newcomers, Carrie began her city life under the roof of a relative, in this case her married sister. Through Carrie's eyes, we see the shabby working-class district where her sister lived, the cramped third-floor apartment, and the "lean and narrow life" that she knew awaited her if she followed the path that had been laid out for her. When she began looking for work in the factory district, she was repelled by the drudgery and low pay that other young women seemed to be willing to accept. Then, to heighten her frustration, she found herself in the city's most opulent shopping district, just a few blocks away. As Carrie wandered through the magnificent Fair store, she experienced the special poignancy of inequality in the industrial city: less than a mile away stood grim slums and factories, yet here she was, surrounded by a

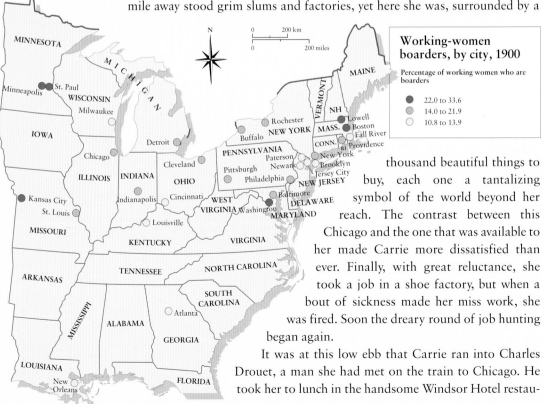

Working-women boarders, by city, 1900

Percentage of working women who are boarders

- 22.0 to 33.6
- 14.0 to 21.9
- 10.8 to 13.9

thousand beautiful things to buy, each one a tantalizing symbol of the world beyond her reach. The contrast between this Chicago and the one that was available to her made Carrie more dissatisfied than ever. Finally, with great reluctance, she took a job in a shoe factory, but when a bout of sickness made her miss work, she was fired. Soon the dreary round of job hunting began again.

It was at this low ebb that Carrie ran into Charles Drouet, a man she had met on the train to Chicago. He took her to lunch in the handsome Windsor Hotel restaurant and a few days later bought her some clothes at Schlesinger & Mayer. Drouet's beneficence reminds us of the delicate line that young urban women like Carrie walked. On the one hand, they were considerably more independent, both socially and economically, than their mothers' generation. Indeed, the dramatic expansion of urban entertainment facilities during these years (dance halls, vaudeville theaters, restaurants, and amusement parks) was in part a response to the presence of so many young women with at least modest resources of money and leisure. On the other hand, these young women were also more sexually vulnerable than their predecessors. The new urban culture provided far more opportunities for dalliance than earlier generations would have thought proper, and the custom for men (because of their higher earnings) to "treat" women on social evenings could lead very quickly to an expectation of sexual favors in exchange.

Carrie risked more than most young women of her times, and managed to survive all the same. Not long after meeting Drouet, she allowed him to rent a room for her, and soon they took an apartment together, pretending to be man and wife. Perhaps Drouet would ultimately have married her, as he promised, but in the meantime Carrie fell in love with one of his friends, a prosperous married man named George Hurstwood. Her life in Chicago ended, as it had begun, in a railroad station, as she prepared to run off with Hurstwood to start a new life in New York City.

For Carrie, breaking every rule of virtuous behavior worked out quite well, both in Chicago and later in New York, where, while Hurstwood sank into poverty and depression, she found fame and wealth as an actress. But if it is pleasant to watch Carrie break the rules and get away with it, it is also important to remember how rare her case was, and how many more women gambled as she did but lost, or lived all their lives within the narrow range of choices that she managed to escape.

1 Carrie arrives in Chicago. C & N.W. depot.

2 Hansons' apartment. 354 West Van Buren Street.

3 Factory district. Van Buren Street.

4 The Fair department store. State and Adams streets.

5 Shoe factory where Carrie worked. Fifth Ave. and Adams.

6 Windsor Hotel. 143 Dearborn Street.

7 Schlesinger & Mayer's store. 128 State Street.

8 Carrie's rented room. Wabash Ave., near Van Buren St.

9 Carrie and Drouet's apartment. Ogden Place.

10 Carrie leaves Chicago. Michigan Central depot.

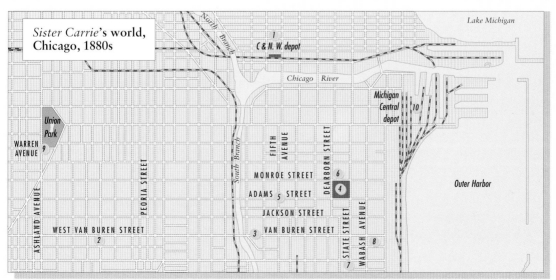

Sister Carrie's world, Chicago, 1880s

New Professional Careers for Women

As late as 1910, college students represented less than 3 percent of the entire population aged 18 to 24. Yet their numbers had more than doubled since the Civil War, and women played an important role in that increase. In 1860, only three private colleges in the country admitted women. Over the next several decades, many coeducational institutions opened and a number of female colleges were established. By 1910, women represented nearly 40 percent of the nation's college enrollment.

Attending college gave young women wider intellectual horizons as well as lifetime membership in a sorority of unusually talented and dedicated women. But it did not provide the same career opportunities that it did for men. In law, for instance, the first white female received her degree in 1870 and the first African-American female in 1872; by 1920 women were accepted by every state bar and most law schools. Yet women remained a small minority of total law school enrollment, and once they graduated, they found many areas of the profession blocked to them. Medicine presented even more obstacles. Women gained early ground in 1849 when Elizabeth Blackwell became the first American woman to earn a medical degree. But by the turn of the century, the drive by leading physicians to strengthen their profession by upgrading medical education had forced the closure of many small schools, including a number founded specifically to train women; most of the new university-based schools accepted only men. Furthermore, as in law, female doctors continued to encounter gender barriers throughout their careers.

Despite these obstacles, the college women of the late nineteenth century did not abandon their goals. Some sought out the areas within established professions that were most accessible to women—practicing family law instead

Colleges admitting women, 1891

•   college

Hospitals training female doctors, 1891

⊕ hospital, with date of founding

New England Hospital
Boston, Massachusetts
1863

New York Infirmary
New York
1857

Woman's Hospital
Philadelphia, Pennsylvania
1862

Northwestern Hospital
Minneapolis, Minnesota
1882

Woman's Hospital
Chicago, Illinois
1865

Hospital for Sick Children and Women
San Francisco, California
1875

0   300 km

0   300 miles

of corporate law, for instance, or teaching children instead of university students. Other female graduates threw themselves into social reform. The expanding field of nursing also opened new careers for women; in Pennsylvania alone, 120 nursing schools were established between 1890 and 1910. Nurses were not required to have college degrees, but those who did became the leaders of the new profession, directing its training and taking the field in new directions such as public-health nursing.

This generation of educated women broke new ground as workers and they were also pioneers in their private lives. They understood the obligations that marriage placed on women and they recognized that it would be extraordinarily difficult to combine those obligations with careers. Weighing the options, an unprecedented number of these college graduates—nearly half—chose to remain single. Some made their way on their own; others shared their lives with other women, combining emotional attachment and professional fulfillment in a way that few marriages of the time would have permitted. These female college graduates were often dismissed as spinsterish bluestockings, yet the contemporary images of a more independent American woman—the insouciant Gibson Girl, the intrepid lady bicyclist, the selfsufficient "bachelor girl"—owed a good deal to their pioneering example.

Visiting nurses like this one, photographed in New York City in 1910, brought health services directly to the homes of the poorest immigrant families.

Women and Progressive-Era Reform

The Progressive Era, as much as any other time in American history, was a period whose fundamental character was defined by women as well as men. During these years (roughly 1890 to 1917), people operating from many different perspectives and through many different organizations struggled to improve American society. Women led some of these movements and participated in virtually all of them.

As early as 1879, Frances Willard, the president of the Women's Christian Temperance Union, instituted a "Do-Everything Policy," which led the organization to concern itself with social issues ranging from pornography to women's suffrage to factory conditions. The WCTU more or less returned to its focus on prohibition after Willard's departure in the 1890s, but by then a new center of reform energy was emerging: the settlement movement.

Its most charismatic leader was Jane Addams, a member of the redoubtable generation of college graduates described in the previous section. Addams was

Hull House,
Chicago,
1889–1916

building
yard

troubled by the bitter labor conflicts of the times and concerned about the growing gulf between her own middle class and the immigrants who were crowding into America's cities. Building on work she had seen in London, in 1889 she bought a house in one of Chicago's poorest immigrant communities and established it as Hull House, offering a range of social and cultural services for the neighborhood. The staff consisted of college graduates who made a personal commitment to the neighborhood by living at the house as well as working there. By 1910 there were 400 settlements around the country. Female volunteers commonly outnumbered males in these institutions, and women often served as chief administrators.

The settlement workers were not immune to the prejudices of their class. Most either neglected African Americans or served them in segregated locations, while programs for immigrants frequently stressed transforming them into "real" Americans rather than valuing their own traditions. Nevertheless, settlement workers introduced an impressive array of new urban services, including clean-milk stations, well-baby clinics, cultural and recreational programs, kindergartens, and community kitchens. Some of the most progressive leaders like Addams went further, making their institutions into bases for agitation for improved housing, safer factories, union organizing, juvenile justice, and ending child labor. These women also helped move the federal government toward a more activist role in social issues, most notably with the formation of the U.S. Children's Bureau in 1912, headed by a Hull House veteran, Julia Lathrop.

Women's clubs provided another important base for female reform. By 1900 the largest network, the General Federation of Women's Clubs, had more than 150,000 members. Most of the clubs in the GFWC had initially been founded as cultural and recreational organizations, but during the Progressive Era they became more activist, supporting libraries, children's clinics, schools, and settlements, and providing influential advocacy for such causes as conservation, pure food and drugs, the abolition of child labor, and woman suffrage. In the African-American community, the National Association of Colored Women, as well as many smaller women's organizations, worked for a similar variety of educational and social reforms; they also promoted one cause on which most women's clubs remained silent: the need for racial justice.

ILLINOIS

Rockford
Ladies Civic and Social Club, 1904
Nonpareil Club, 1909

Evanston
Julia Gaston Club, 1898

Chicago

Hallie Quinn Brown Club, 1904
Art and Study Club, 1913

Moline

Rock Island
Progressive Art Club, 1910

Braidwood
Sojourner Truth Club, 1914

Galesburg
Autumn Leaf Club, 1890
Woman's Progressive Club, 1909
Phillis Wheatley Club, 1910

Peoria
Peoria Woman's Aid Club, 1899

Canton
Woman's Auxiliary Club, 1913

Bloomington
Colored Woman's Club, 1901
Domestic Art Club, 1915

Springfield Colored Woman's Club, 1899
Springfield

Danville
Colored Woman's Aid Club, 1902

Jacksonville
Ladies West Side Art Club, 1914

Decatur
Big Sister's Club, 1913

0   50 km
0   50 miles
N

East St. Louis
Violet Thimble Club, 1916

DuQuoin
Hallie Q. Brown Charity Club, 1908

Yates Woman's Club, 1905

Cairo

Ida B. Wells Club, 1893
Phillis Wheatley Woman's Club, 1896
Woman's Civic League, 1897
Cornell Charity Club, 1902
Volunteer Workers Charity Club, 1904
Imperial Art Club, 1907
Ideal Woman's Club, 1908
Giles Charity Club, 1910
Union Charity Club, 1910
Gaudeamus Charity Club, 1911
Clara Jessamine Club, 1912
East Side Woman's Club, 1912
Young Matron's Culture Club, 1915

Affiliates of the Illinois Federation of Colored Women's Clubs, 1916

□   club, with date of founding

Bohemian Women

*Suffragist and writer
Marie Jenney Howe was
the founder (1912) and
longtime chair of
Heterodoxy, a Greenwich
Village "club for
unorthodox women."*

When people spoke of the "New Woman" in the early twentieth century, they were responding to trends that were observable in many American communities: the fact that more young women were going about unchaperoned, living alone or with female friends, speaking out on public issues, and exchanging corsets and trailing gowns for natural waists and ankle-length skirts. Working-class women had prepared the ground by helping to foster a culture of public recreation so free and lively that it attracted participants from the middle class as well. Female professionals had opened other possibilities by building distinguished careers instead of marrying. A third set of pioneers was the group of women who chose to live in a free-spirited style that came to be known as "Bohemian."

Between 1900 and 1914 many of these young Bohemians gravitated to New York and settled in Greenwich Village, then an impoverished ethnic neighborhood. There these artists, writers, and political radicals built a community that would attract cultural rebels for decades to come. For women, Village life offered not only the opportunity to break new ground professionally, but also the chance to share ideas with like-minded people and to form sexual relationships outside marriage with the man or woman of one's choice. Many noteworthy careers began in the Village during these years. For example, within a few blocks of each other, Willa Cather wrote several major novels, Edna St. Vincent Millay established herself as a poet, Gertrude Vanderbilt Whitney started her work as a sculptor and art patron, and Crystal Eastman moved from law school to a career in social advocacy.

Greenwich Village women participated in many collaborative efforts, including art galleries, experimental theater companies, elaborate costume balls, political rallies, labor protests, and a host of "little magazines." One of the most important women's institutions was the Heterodoxy Club, founded in 1912 with a membership of feminists, labor organizers, political radicals, and professionals. Each biweekly meeting began with lunch at Polly's, a favorite Village restaurant that was run by an ebullient woman whose anarchist lover served as cook and waiter. Afterward everyone, including Polly, adjourned upstairs to debate politics, philosophy, women's rights, birth control, pacifism, and a host of other topics. The wealthy Mabel Dodge, a Heterodoxy member, maintained her own Village institution—a salon that attracted a heady mixture of artists, writers, reformers, labor leaders, radicals, and socialites.

Dodge's life had been transformed by living in Paris for several years, where she had met many American expatriate women, most notably Gertrude Stein and Alice B. Toklas. Her experience reminds us that New York was not the only city where American women were building lives based on artistic and sexual freedom. To recognize the scope of the movement, we need only think of Isadora Duncan, who during these years took her pathbreaking vision of modern dance from San Francisco to Paris to Moscow, leaving stunned audiences and a number of lovers in her wake. Wherever these Bohemian women found themselves, the way they lived and worked broadened still further the sense of what a woman might do with her life.

> **Landmarks of Bohemian life in Greenwich Village, 1910–25**
>
> ★   residence
>
> ★   social life
>
> ★   arts and politics

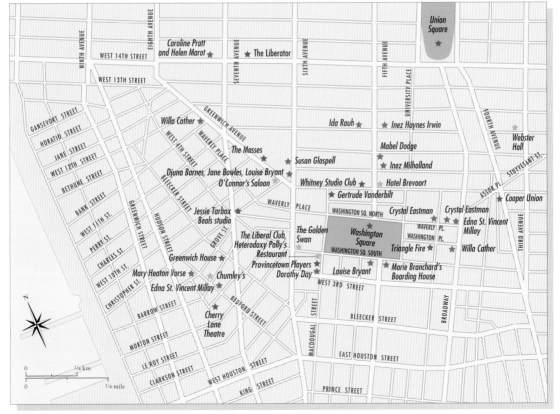

PART IV: TWO STEPS FORWARD, ONE STEP BACKWARD: 1914–1965

As 1914 began, most Americans must have expected that the years ahead would bring the same gradual expansion of opportunities for women that had occurred in recent decades. Occupational doors were continuing to open, woman suffrage was making headway, World War I was not yet on the horizon, and it must have seemed reasonable to expect a continuation of the social trends that had shaped American life since the late nineteenth century.

In fact, events followed quite a difference course. Between 1914 and 1965 the United States experienced a succession of cataclysmic national and international events, including two world wars, the greatest economic depression in American history, and an extended Cold War with the Soviet Union. In this climactic atmosphere, the question of women's status in society commanded far less attention than it had in the recent past. The years between 1914 to 1965 did include several periods during which women assumed significant new responsibilities, but each was followed by a period of reaction, during which traditional gender roles were reaffirmed. As for women's activism on their own behalf, once suffrage was won in 1920, 45 years would pass before another broad-based movement emerged whose first priority was to increase opportunities for women.

The most significant expansion of female roles occurred during the two world wars. During World War I, female enlistees were accepted for the first time by both the Navy and the Marines. Their numbers were small and most of them performed only clerical duties, but their presence established an important precedent for World War II, when every major service created a female branch. During that war nearly 400,000 women enlisted, and they were assigned to an extraordinarily broad range of jobs. Despite pervasive gender distinctions, military duty introduced women to new occupations, the experience of command, and the pride of serving their country in a way that few women had done before.

Working in defense industries represented another kind of new horizon for women. In both world wars, jobs that had long been described as too difficult for women began opening up once the men marched away. During World War I, because the peak period of production was relatively brief, most defense jobs went to young single women who were already in the workforce. But during World War II millions of additional women were recruited. Just as in the military, female defense workers encountered considerable gender discrimination, yet most women appear to have enjoyed the challenge, good wages, and sense of usefulness that they got from their wartime jobs. Indeed, many expressed resentment when they were let go to make way for the returning soldiers.

During the 1930s, women enlisted in another kind of struggle against the hardship engendered by the Great Depression. This time, the problem was not too many jobs, but too few. With so many people looking for work, businesses and government offices often refrained from hiring women or singled them out for dismissal because of the widespread belief that only male workers had to support families. Yet many women did continue to work and some became their families' only breadwinners. Women also assumed family leadership in other ways: taking the lead in seeking the charity help their husbands could not bear to ask for and holding their households together while their husbands traveled across the country looking for work.

When women take on new responsibilities, the social impact of their changed role is strongly influenced by the way their behavior is interpreted by their contemporaries. With respect to women's activities during the Depression and the two world wars, one theme dominated the public response: the idea that in assuming new tasks, women were functioning as gallant but temporary substitutes for men. However much praise was heaped on the wife struggling to support her family during the Depression or Rosie the Riveter building an airplane in World War II, the interpretation reiterated by government and the media was that these new roles were temporary. When things returned to "normal," men would start doing their regular jobs again and women could go back to depending on them.

Black nurses like these, based in Australia in 1944, won the right to serve their country only after tireless advocacy by supporters like Mabel K. Staupers and the National Association of Colored Graduate Nurses.

This interpretation helped promote a rapid return to more familiar gender roles as soon as each world war ended. In the 1920s, and even more dramatically during the 1950s, homemaking was once again presented as women's only truly satisfying occupation. Indeed, during the 1950s the image of the "typical" American family with Mom safe in her suburban kitchen became an icon of Cold War rhetoric, adding the force of patriotism to the familiar emphasis on women's domestic obligations. Working mothers were rarely portrayed in the media, a practice that effectively hid from view the experience of huge numbers of women—particularly African Americans and Latinas, but also a growing proportion of white women. Nor did the country make much progress toward gender equality in the workplace: As late as 1965, female wage levels remained significantly below men's, well-paid factory work had reverted to being a male preserve, women were still underrepresented in the upper levels of every profession, and the proportion of doctorates granted to women was actually lower than in 1920.

The decades preceding 1914 had represented a fairly steady expansion of the opportunities open to women. The next 50 years followed a much more erratic pattern, combining periods of significant change with other periods during which old patterns were vigorously reinforced. By the mid-1960s, women's growing dissatisfaction with the status quo, combined with the energizing example of the Civil Rights Movement, had begun to set the stage for the revival of American feminism.

Winning the Vote

The first time that American women formally demanded the right to vote was at the Seneca Falls Convention on women's rights in 1848. More than 70 years would pass before the nation granted that demand, and racial discrimination at the state level would force most southern black women to wait even longer, until the Voting Rights Act of 1965. Besides race prejudice, a major reason for the long delay was the idea (held by many women as well as men) that politics did not fit the female character. Some believed women were too dependent on men to cast an independent vote; others thought their purity would be sullied by the rough-and-tumble of politics.

Until the Civil War, women's rights advocates gave most of their energies to the crusade for abolition, believing their turn would come next. Once abolition was achieved, however, their male allies argued that the more important drive for black male suffrage must not be jeopardized by including women. Female suffragists themselves divided over the point so bitterly that the movement split in two. One group, the American Woman Suffrage Association, accepted the men's decision; the other, the National Woman Suffrage Association, fought for several years to include women in the Fifteenth Amendment. Even after this battle was lost, the movement remained divided, and woman suffrage encountered repeated defeats in state referenda. Some suffragists tried to vote in the 1872 presidential election, maintaining that as American citizens they did not need new legislation, but the Supreme Court rejected that argument. By 1890, women were allowed to participate in local or school elections in 19 states, but they had full voting equality in only Wyoming.

The suffrage movement took on new life after 1890, starting when its warring factions finally reunited in the

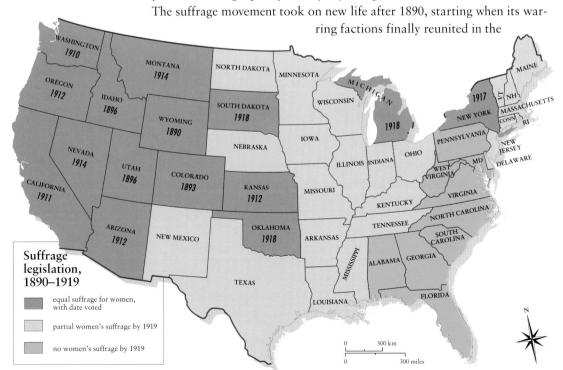

Suffrage legislation, 1890–1919

- equal suffrage for women, with date voted
- partial women's suffrage by 1919
- no women's suffrage by 1919

0   300 km
0   300 miles

National American Woman Suffrage Association. During these years, the movement lost its two founders, Elizabeth Cady Stanton and Susan B. Anthony, but the surge in women's organizations during the Progressive Era created new opportunities for women to demonstrate their civic power, and many of these organizations lent their support to suffrage, either because they felt that women were as good as men, or because they felt they were spiritually better and could purify politics. The movement did have its less creditable features. Its white leaders showed little solidarity with the lively black suffragist movement, and they were not above suggesting that letting white women vote would help offset the votes of male blacks and immigrants. On the other hand, the movement did become more inclusive in terms of class after the turn of the century, drawing thousands of wage-earning women into the struggle.

Gradually, NAWSA built a formidable network of state associations, while the more radical National Women's Party launched a series of militant protests in Washington, D.C., including hunger strikes and picketing the White House. One after another, the western states began granting women the vote, and in 1917 New York gave the movement its first eastern victory for full suffrage, followed by Michigan a year later. Women in the remaining states won the vote when the Nineteenth Amendment to the U.S. Constitution passed Congress in 1919 and was ratified in 1920.

Vote on woman suffrage in New York state, 1917

In percent

- 58 to 65
- 54 to 57
- 50 to 53
- 47 to 49
- 43 to 46
- 32 to 42

Vote on woman suffrage, U.S. House of Representatives, May 21, 1919

- yeas
- nays
- unsettled
- not voting

83

Women in World War I

ILLINOIS

Organize night schools to teach working women (especially immigrants) about food conservation.

Set up driving classes and nurses' training for women.

Promote adequate conditions for women in industry.

GEORGIA

Promote diversified farming rather than cotton production alone.

Organize girls' canning clubs.

Get local artists to perform at Officers Training School camps.

Get state university to open classes to women.

Organize classes for women in stenography, typing, radio operation, map reading, radiology, and driving.

Find homes for servicemen's families.

CALIFORNIA

Campaign to sell Liberty Loan bonds.

Circulate Hoover Food Pledges (by signing, one pledges to conserve food for the war effort).

Research labor supply for farms, to keep farm production steady.

Advocate fair labor standards for women drawn into the workforce.

CONNECTICUT

Promote training of nurses' assistants.

Ensure adequate and wholesome social opportunities on nearby military bases.

Advocate good working conditions for female government workers.

Promote the creation of day nurseries for female defense workers.

World War I opened many nontraditional occupations to women, yet at the same time it accentuated the importance of women's most traditional responsibilities as wives and mothers. One example of the balance between traditional and nontraditional female behavior can be seen in the way that women opposed America's entry into the war.

When the fighting began in Europe in 1914, thousands of women joined the movement to keep the United States out of the hostilities. In publicizing their views, many stressed their traditional identity as wives and mothers, singing songs such as "I Didn't Raise My Boy to Be a Soldier." However, once America came in on the Allied side in 1917, opposition became a controversial political act. Relatively few women continued to speak out against the war, and those who did—such as the anarchist Emma Goldman, the socialist Kate Richards O'Hare, and the progressive Jane Addams—expressed themselves not as women protecting their families but as spokespersons for a broader political vision. These wartime dissenters asked no particular consideration because of their gender, and they received none; in fact, both Goldman and O'Hare served prison terms for speaking against enlistment.

Not many women chose to be political agitators during World War I, but they did move into other nontraditional occupations. With one out of every six male workers having departed for the service, jobs opened up that had long been reserved for men, most notably in factories producing goods for the war. At the peak of wartime production women constituted at least one fifth of the labor force in many industries (such as electrical machinery and aviation) where there had been very few female employees before the war. Women in these jobs nearly always earned less than men, but the work still paid considerably better than traditional female occupations. Even black women, who obtained few of the war-related jobs, improved their status by filling positions whites had left behind, including occupations that had previously been closed to them, such as elevator operators and cafeteria waitresses.

Both the Navy and Marines broke new ground by accepting women into their services, mainly as clerks. Army and Navy nurses assumed a growing role in military hospitals, and at least 22,000 American women served in the European war zone with various private agencies and with the military (as nurses or civilian clerical employees).

Although most married women remained outside the labor force just as in peacetime, huge numbers of them supported the war effort as volunteers, working in an elaborate network of state and local associations to conserve food, sell Liberty Bonds, and sustain the home front in other ways. They also struggled to make ends meet during a period of galloping inflation. During 1917, the period when food prices rose the fastest, some housewives took their protest to the streets, attacking stores and even battling the police. In New York City, for example, neighborhood women picketed a number of stores, physically prevented people from shopping there, held rallies at City Hall, and at least temporarily forced the worst offenders among the proprietors to close their doors.

Women workers in the iron and steel industry, 1918

Proportion of women in all wage earners in this industry, in percent

- 65.4
- 25.0
- 10.0
- 5.0
- 1.9
- 0.0

    no data

Washington, D.C.

NAVY, March 1917:
The U.S. Navy authorizes the enrollment of "yeomen (F)," soon called yeomanettes. Approximately 12,500 serve.

CONGRESS, April 6, 1917:
When the House of Representatives approves America's entry into WWI, Jeannette Rankin, the first woman elected to Congress, is one of 50 members who vote no.

MARINES, August 1918 (three months before the end of the war):
The U.S. Marine Corps authorizes enrolling "marines (F)," primarily for clerical work. Approximately 300 serve.

U.S. women's participation in World War I

    U.S. territory

American Samoa

Pearl Harbor — PACIFIC OCEAN — Wake Is.

Hawaii — Midway Is.

Female members of the U.S. Naval Reserve

Guam

Female members of the U.S. Naval Reserve

JAPANESE EMPIRE

Philippines

Alaska

CANADA

UNITED STATES

MEXICO

Arctic Circle

UNITED KINGDOM — GERMANY — FRANCE — SPAIN — OTTOMAN EMPIRE

Female members of the U.S. Naval Reserve

Panama

Puerto Rico

Female members of the U.S. Naval Reserve

COLOMBIA — VENEZUELA

BRAZIL

ATLANTIC OCEAN

French West Africa

EUROPE

Estimated total U.S. women working in Europe during WWI: at least 22,000, associated with more than 50 American agencies and 45 foreign ones. These include:

ARMY: about 1,300 female civilians work with the Signal Corps, the Quartermaster Corps, Ordnance, Treasury Dept., and Secret Services.

ARMY AND NAVY NURSES: more than 10,000

RED CROSS RELIEF: about 4,600

YMCA: about 3,500 (including more than 500 entertainers)

YWCA: about 430

SALVATION ARMY: about 110

AMERICAN WOMEN'S HOSPITALS: 350 female doctors

QUAKERS: about 50

Women's Politics after Suffrage

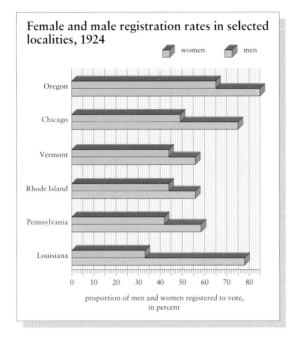

Female and male registration rates in selected localities, 1924

women ▢   men ▢

Oregon
Chicago
Vermont
Rhode Island
Pennsylvania
Louisiana

0 10 20 30 40 50 60 70 80

proportion of men and women registered to vote, in percent

By the end of 1920, two dreams long cherished by American women had been achieved: national alcohol prohibition and women's suffrage. For years, many women had believed that these changes would usher in an era of unprecedented social progress building on and expanding the reforms won during the Progressive Era. The reality was less utopian.

Prohibition did lower drinking rates to some extent, but the pervasive presence of bootlegging, speakeasies, and drinking in private homes made clear how little of a dent had been made in the overall problem and how disinclined public officials were to take the matter further. Additionally, the presence of women in the electorate seemed to have little impact on the enforcement of Prohibition or on any other issue. Despite organizations such as the new League of Women Voters and a network of state-level women's legislative councils, women's turnout rates were low and their pattern of electoral choices hardly different from men's.

Women's limited use of their voting power was part of a broader social pattern. During the 1920s many Americans of both sexes seemed to narrow their focus to the comfort and security of their own families. Some may have been reacting to the losses and disillusionments of the recent war and to the considerable prosperity that the new decade ushered in. Others may have been influenced by the ferocious backlash against radicalism of all kinds that followed a series of strikes in 1919. Weighing their personal gains against the growing costs of activism, many Americans seem to have found private life more appealing than trying to save the world. The retreat from reform was reflected in the organizational life of American women. Victory had dissipated two of the most vibrant centers of female activity—the temperance movement and the suffrage movement.

Women's peace organizations between the wars

National Women's Congress on the Cause and Cure of War
Peace Committee of the National Council of Jewish Women
Woman's Pro-League Council
Women's Church Committee on International Good Will
Women's Committee for World Disarmament
Women's Council for the Prevention of War
Women's International League for Peace and Freedom
Women's Nonpartisan Committee for the League of Nations
Women's Peace Society
Women's Peace Union
Women's World Disarmament Committee

Meanwhile, those groups that continued to function, such as the General Federation of Women's Clubs, virtually abandoned their previous pioneering programs and began to focus on less controversial topics such as fighting pornography and promoting home economics.

The decade was not without its political and social achievements. Thanks to the leadership of the new U.S. Women's Bureau, the Sheppard-Towner Act broke new ground by providing federal funds for maternal and child health-care services, even though conservatives killed the program in 1929. In the South, black and white women took the first steps toward dialogue in a network of committees organized by the Commission on Interracial Cooperation, and in 1930 a group of southern white women launched their own crusade against lynching—a crime that black women had been protesting for decades, and one that in the past had often been rationalized as necessary to protect white women's honor.

Women also played a major role in the peace movement, supported the campaign for birth control, and helped start innovative social programs at the state level that would provide models for the later New Deal. Yet many of the leaders of these activities were vilified by right-wing critics as Communists and traitors. Even the long-sought constitutional amendment outlawing child labor, passed by Congress in 1924, failed to achieve ratification in the states. Overall, the 1920s did not represent the level of national progress for which many earlier activists had hoped.

Black Women Leaving the South

Between 1914 and 1925, one of American history's great internal population movements occurred—the migration of about 1.5 million African Americans from southern rural areas to cities in the North and in California. There were good economic reasons for the move, since most of the migrants were impoverished sharecroppers. In addition, southern segregation—by then fully in place—constrained black lives with its rigid laws and periodic violence.

World War I opened up a host of jobs in northern industrial cities as well as in Los Angeles and San Francisco, and while the best of these jobs were closed to blacks (particularly to black women), the booming wartime economy meant that the newcomers were at least in demand to fill the less desirable positions vacated by whites. Between 1910 and 1920, Chicago's black population increased by 150 percent, Cleveland's by 300 percent, and Detroit's by 600 percent.

Women represented a minority in the great migration, but their lives were deeply affected by it. Those who remained in the South faced the challenge of managing on their own—in some cases, for the rest of their lives. The several hundred thousand women who did make the journey faced other challenges. Having spent their whole lives on southern farms, they struggled to adapt to crowded tenements, noisy streets, and northern winters. Moreover, racial separation was nearly as pervasive in the rest of the country as in the South, though it was less formal. African Americans found themselves relegated to the poorest housing and most menial occupations, while the resentment of local working-class whites provoked a number of ugly race riots between 1917 and 1919.

Yet if these cities were no paradise, few black women chose to go back to the South. Even after the wartime boom ended,

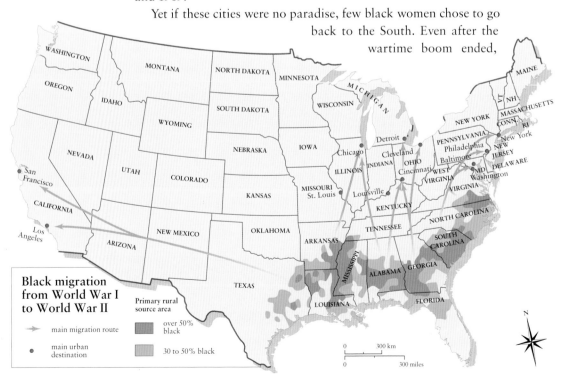

Black migration from World War I to World War II

→ main migration route

● main urban destination

Primary rural source area

over 50% black

30 to 50% black

their economic chances were better than at home. Moreover, the new urban black communities developed their own vibrant culture. The jazz that the migrants brought with them became enormously popular, and even though racial discrimination blocked singers such as Bessie Smith, Ethel Waters, and Florence Mills from many of the opportunities they should have enjoyed, they did achieve considerable recognition for their work.

Meanwhile, middle-class northern blacks began to show new interest in their racial heritage, expressed most notably in the Harlem Renaissance—a movement of artists and writers that fostered and celebrated black culture. Men dominated this circle, as they did the jazz world, but many gifted women contributed their work to the cultural ferment, including Zora Neale Hurston, Alice Dunbar Nelson, Jessie Redmon Fauset, and Nella Larsen. In other segments of the black community, Amy Jacques Garvey played a vital role in her husband Marcus' Universal Negro Improvement Association, while Madame C.J. Walker made her fortune and created many jobs for the black community by developing beauty products for African-American women.

Churchgoers and jazz singers, writers and household maids—black women born in the South played an important role in reshaping the urban culture of 1920s America.

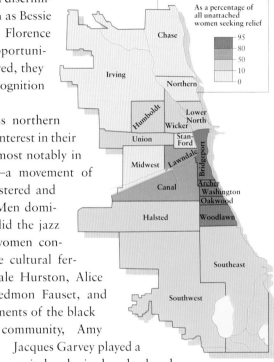

Black "unattached women" seeking relief, Chicago, 1936

As a percentage of all unattached women seeking relief

- 95
- 80
- 50
- 10
- 0

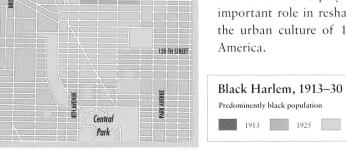

Black Harlem, 1913–30

Predominently black population

- 1913
- 1925
- 1930

Women's Work between the Wars

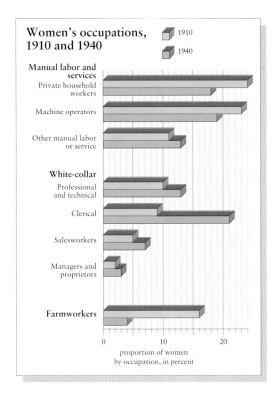

Women's occupations, 1910 and 1940

1910
1940

Manual labor and services
Private household workers

Machine operators

Other manual labor or service

White-collar
Professional and technical

Clerical

Salesworkers

Managers and proprietors

Farmworkers

0   10   20
proportion of women by occupation, in percent

The greatest change in women's employment between 1910 and 1940 was the growing number of women in white-collar occupations. Other patterns remained quite stable: The percentage of women who had jobs increased only slightly (from about 25 percent to 27), and, as in the past, the majority of working women were single. But between 1910 and 1940, the proportion of women doing white-collar jobs rose from a quarter to nearly half. The opening up of these opportunities for women reflected the growing importance in the American economy of services such as sales, education, communications, medical care, banking, insurance, and entertainment. It also reflected the reduction of immigration after World War I. As the expansion of service jobs outran the supply of available males, women were called on to fill the gap.

White-collar work for women rarely meant careers as lawyers or business executives; more commonly, it involved low-paid jobs as school teachers and secretaries. Even when women moved into tasks formerly assigned to men, the effect was generally to lower the prestige of the jobs rather than to raise the prestige of the women. For example, clerical positions had often represented—for men— the first rung on the business career ladder. But as these occupations became feminized, their salary levels declined and their link to advancement disappeared. Once that happened, few men chose to enter these fields; by 1940, women accounted for more than 90 percent of the workforce in such occupations as librarian, nurse, telephone operator, and stenographer.

Working wives and widows in Philadelphia, 1925

Neighborhood	Description	Proportion of wives and widows who worked	Usual women's jobs	Ethnicity of working women
Kensington	Heavily industrial	24.9%	Factory jobs	Native-born, some north European
Northeast	Many factories	20.4%	Domestic service	Mostly Poles
Manayunk	Self-contained settlement on river	23.5%	Factory jobs and managing own small shops	Immigrants from southeast Europe
Southwest	Slum, some industry	15.3%	Factory jobs, domestics, 12% retail or clerical	Native-born, some Irish and black
Northwest	Residential, a few factories	19.0%	Factory jobs, domestics, 18% retail or clerical	Native-born, some Irish and black
Southeast	River wharves, warehouses, cigar factory	15.4%	Factory jobs and managing own small shops	40% immigrants, mostly Poles

Manayunk

Kensington
Northwest   Northeast

Southeast
Southwest

Despite the expansion of white-collar jobs, the majority of America's working women still earned their living in service and manufacturing jobs. (As an example, note the pattern of female employment in the accompanying chart for five Philadelphia neighborhoods in 1925.) In fact the absolute number of women holding service and manufacturing jobs actually increased between 1910 and 1940. But because that number grew more slowly than the population, it represented a smaller proportion of all women's employment. Two regional trends emerged. In the North, the number of white women willing to enter domestic service grew steadily smaller, partly because there were fewer new immigrants and partly because of the growing opportunities in other fields; this opened many more domestic service jobs to black women. In the South, a tremendous expansion of the textile industry led many women (mostly white) to move from agriculture to factory work.

The issue of whether female workers required special protection against long hours and dangerous conditions became the focus of a corrosive battle among women's advocates. Many believed that female workers required "protective legislation"; some also felt that winning these rights for women could pave the way to improving conditions for all workers. However, the National Woman's Party and other dissenters argued that protective legislation made it more expensive to hire women and therefore disadvantaged them in the job market. In the long run, these advocates argued, women would gain more from equality than from special protection. The proponents of protective legislation generally prevailed during the 1920s and 1930s, but the question would continue to concern (and divide) female activists for decades to come.

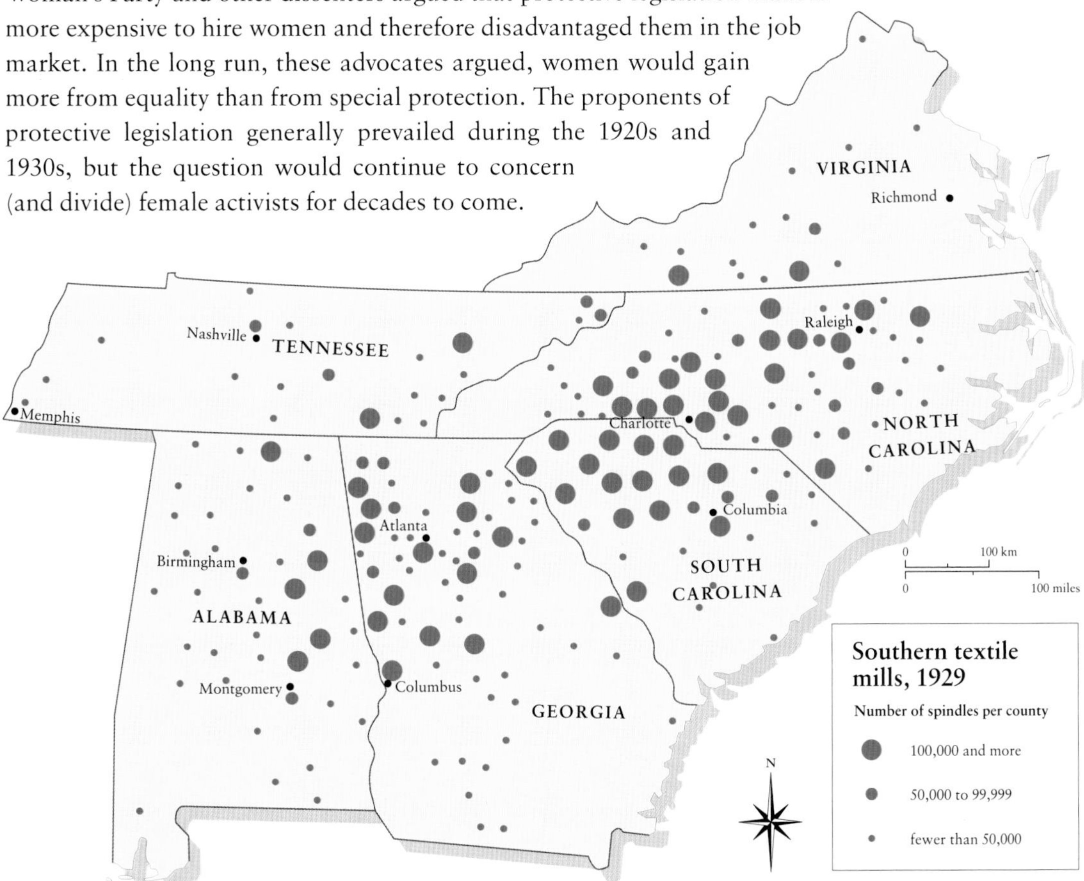

Southern textile mills, 1929

Number of spindles per county

- ● 100,000 and more
- ● 50,000 to 99,999
- · fewer than 50,000

A World of Things to Buy

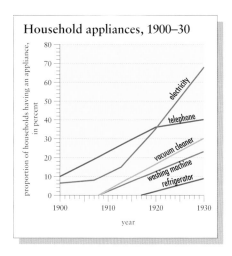

Household appliances, 1900–30

During the 1920s there was a dramatic increase in the volume and variety of mass-produced consumer goods. Widely promoted and widely accepted, these products helped to redefine popular ideas about what constituted the "average" American family way of life.

Perhaps none of the new products was embraced more enthusiastically than the automobile. Henry Ford's production innovations made cars affordable for Americans of nearly every class; by 1930, car registrations had already reached 20 million. Families of even modest means started taking vacation trips by car; a new cluster of "automobile suburbs" began to emerge beyond and between the trolley lines; and young people took joyful advantage of the independence and privacy that the car provided. Poor urban families bought few cars, but farmers acquired Model T trucks in record numbers, to their wives' delight. One such woman, offered her choice between a bathtub and a truck, chose the latter. "You can't go to town in a bathtub," she explained.

By 1929, two thirds of American homes had electricity. As electric motors were developed small enough for home use and other technologies became more refined, a great variety of home appliances began to appear on the market. Some, such as the radio, appealed to the whole family, but many—such as electric stoves, refrigerators, washing machines, vacuum cleaners, toasters, and irons—were used primarily by housewives. With this new equipment, it was possible to cook a meal without carrying wood or coal; to keep food fresh without maintaining a supply of ice; to wash clothes without toiling over a tub; to clean house more efficiently than with a broom; and to do one's ironing without the discomfort, heavy lifting, and uneven heat of the old flatirons.

Families having a radio, 1930

In percent

64
50
42
27
5

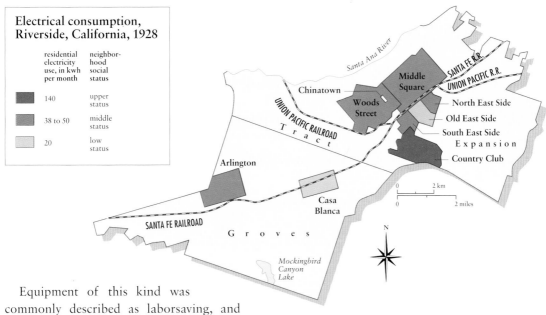

Electrical consumption, Riverside, California, 1928

residential electricity use, in kwh per month	neighborhood social status
140	upper status
38 to 50	middle status
20	low status

Equipment of this kind was commonly described as laborsaving, and indeed it was, although in many cases the labor saved was that of the domestic servants who had done the work before. Most wealthy families continued to employ household help during the 1920s, but by this time a smaller proportion of the female workforce was entering domestic service. Responding to what was widely described as "the servant problem," many middle-class housewives began to settle for day workers or weekly cleaning women instead of the live-in help they had been accustomed to in the past. Filling in the gaps, they began to do more of their own housework, a change that was facilitated by the new electrical equipment.

Working-class housewives stood to gain the most from the new appliances since they had always maintained their own homes, but their access was more limited. (For instance, on the accompanying map of Riverside, California, note how much less electricity low-status neighborhoods used, compared to high-status neighborhoods.) The poorest families, particularly in rural areas, often had no electricity at all. Nevertheless, all women's lives were affected by the changes under way. As the expanding field of advertising spread images of the new consumer goods nationwide, it fostered the idea that having a car, a radio, a washing machine, and a refrigerator was fundamental to being a "real" American housewife.

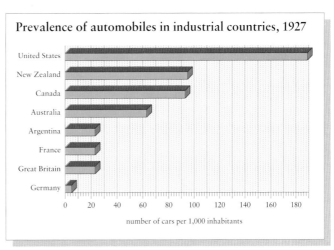

Prevalence of automobiles in industrial countries, 1927

number of cars per 1,000 inhabitants

Selling Beauty

Women became important consumers of commercially advertised commodities during the 1920s. At the same time, they became commodities themselves, in the sense that a growing portion of American commerce turned on displaying pretty young women for profit.

A number of trends contributed to this development. First, advertising and public relations expanded dramatically, and with them the use of attractive young women as promotional images. For instance, when the Miss America pageant was launched in 1921, it was presented as a high-minded tribute to unspoiled American womanhood. Yet this event was fundamentally nothing

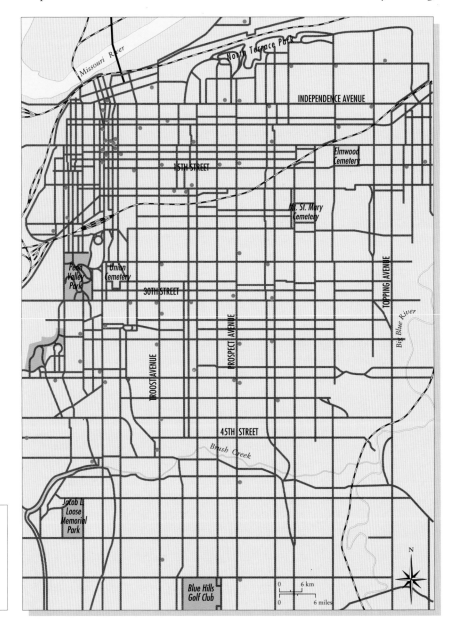

Movie theaters in Kansas City, Missouri, 1928

●   movie theater

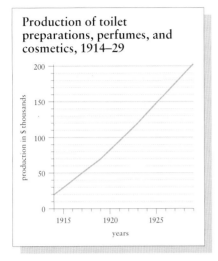

Production of toilet preparations, perfumes, and cosmetics, 1914–29

more elevated than a bathing-suit competition designed to encourage tourism in Atlantic City after Labor Day. Promotions based on women's looks continued to expand throughout the 1920s, most notably in industries such as cosmetics and fashion.

Women's looks were also a valuable commodity in the burgeoning film industry. The movies had begun as a somewhat disreputable amusement for working-class immigrants but during the 1920s they developed into a major entertainment medium for Americans of all classes. Dazzling movie palaces drew huge audiences, particularly after "talking pictures" were introduced in 1927. By 1930, the average weekly audience hovered near 80 million. (To understand the impact at the local level, see the accompanying map, which shows that in 1928 even a modest-size city such as Kansas City, Missouri, had more than 50 downtown movie theaters.) Men held commanding positions in the film industry as studio heads, producers, and directors, but in the one occupation where physical appearance mattered—performing—the top female stars not only equaled men's earning power but outdid them, a pattern not to be found in any other industry at that time. No one would suggest that stars such as Mary Pickford and Gloria Swanson achieved their fame on looks alone. Nevertheless, it is clear that their careers were built at least in part on their looks, as were the careers of many lesser female performers who embellished the comedies, romances, and adventure stories that held movie audiences spellbound.

Adding edge to the marketing of female beauty during the 1920s was the growing sexual openness of the times. Illicit sex remained nearly as taboo as before, but the short skirts of the 1920s flapper, her rouged cheeks, bobbed hair, frenetic dancing, and easy flirtations set a tone that contrasted strongly with the proprieties of her mother's generation. When these were combined with the disappearance of chaperones, the backstreet excitement of Prohibition, and the sketchily understood teachings of Sigmund Freud, they produced an atmosphere that lent a hint of sexual allure to the picture of any young woman, however pure.

The increasing commercial use of feminine beauty during the 1920s was a mixed blessing for women. On the one hand, it opened new female careers, some of which led to stunning financial success. On the other hand, it reinforced the concept that women were to be judged primarily by their appearance. This idea diminished many women's own sense of themselves and in a larger sense it impoverished the whole society.

Weekly salaries of Famous Players–Lasky's top movie stars 1923

Norma Talmadge	$10,000
Dorothy Dalton	$7,500
Gloria Swanson	$6,500
Larry Semon	$5,000
Constance Talmadge	$5,000
Pauline Frederick	$5,000
Lillian Gish	$5,000
Tom Mix	$4,000
Betty Compson	$3,500
Barbara La Marr	$3,500
May McAvoy	$3,000
Mabel Normand	$3,000
Priscilla Dean	$3,000
Conway Tearle	$2,750
Lewis Stone	$2,500

Women during the Depression

Usual occupations of unemployed women seeking relief, 1933

Usual occupation, with proportion in percent

- domestic, personal service
- factory work
- clerical
- professional
- other

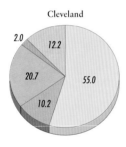

Chicago

14.9
3.6
9.9
18.6
53.0

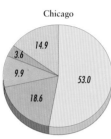

Cleveland

2.0
12.2
20.7
10.2
55.0

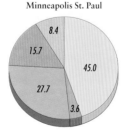

Minneapolis St. Paul

8.4
15.7
27.7
3.6
45.0

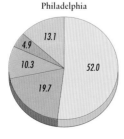

Philadelphia

13.1
4.9
10.3
19.7
52.0

Two or three of the most haunting photographs from the era of the Great Depression are portraits of women pictured on their desolate Dust Bowl farms. But the great majority of familiar Depression images are of men—men lining up at urban soup kitchens, building bridges for the WPA, crossing the country in boxcars looking for work, battling police on the picket line. Even at the time, observers commented on how rarely one saw women in the places where the needy congregated. "Yet," as one reporter commented, "there must be as many women out of jobs in cities and suffering extreme poverty as there are men. What happens to them? Where do they go?"

The reporter was correct that women, like men, were acutely affected by the Depression. They experienced about the same rate of unemployment as men, and in some states such as Pennsylvania the female unemployment rate rose even higher, hitting 31 percent in 1934, compared to 27 percent for men. Clerical workers, teachers, sales clerks, and factory operatives all faced layoffs, while domestic service was hit particularly hard. Yet a mixture of pride and fear kept women out of many of the locations where unemployed men gathered during these years: flophouses, railroad boxcars, soup kitchens, and hobo shantytowns.

Single women scrambled desperately to support themselves

during the Depression, and many married women started looking for work when their husbands lost their jobs. By 1936, a survey of one group of female workers in New York State found that more than 20 percent were the sole support of their families. Yet women continued to be paid less than men because of the continuing perception that only male workers had family obligations. The same assumption led most state and federal work-relief programs to concentrate on creating jobs for men.

The federal programs instituted under President Franklin Roosevelt's New Deal also had other limits as far as women were concerned. Social Security initially excluded several major categories of women's employment, including domestic service. In addition, thousands of women were among the southern sharecroppers who lost their livelihoods when the New Deal began paying farm owners to let their land lie fallow.

Despite these drawbacks, many women did benefit from the New Deal. Roosevelt placed more women in senior administrative positions than any previous president. The Rural Electrification Administration transformed the lives

Minimum wage laws for women and minors, 1937

mandatory law, rates fixed by a commission

rate fixed by law

no law

of an entire generation of farm wives by bringing electricity to more than 900,000 rural homes by 1941. The New Deal's support for labor unions also meant a great deal to women. Some benefited directly as union members; other women—the wives and daughters of workers—provided crucial support during the great strikes of the period and shared in the benefits when victories were won. As for the Works Progress Administration, although it concentrated primarily on male employment, it did provide jobs for more than half a million women. Besides sewing and domestic service, female WPA workers served as librarians and public health nurses, produced public art and dramatic programs, and helped prepare a distinguished series of state guidebooks.

Opposite page.

This southern woman, dispossessed by drought and hard times, was photographed by Dorothea Lange in a California camp for migrant laborers in 1936.

Women's unemployment, by state, 1940

Proportion of unemployed in female labor force aged 14 and over, in percent

13.8
9.5
8.2
7.4
4.5

Eleanor Roosevelt, Voice of Conscience

Eleanor Roosevelt, shown here with labor and civil rights leader A. Philip Randolph, made special efforts to reach out to African Americans, women, and young people.

Picture a train racing through the darkness. Most of the passengers are sleeping, but one woman is sitting erect in the lighted window. As the miles rush by, she works busily on the papers before her, drafting her daily newspaper column, writing letters, reading reports, and going over her notes for tomorrow's speeches. Next morning, when the train pulls into the station, she warmly greets a welcoming deputation and kneels down to receive a child's gift of flowers. By the time the group has piled into cars for the day's round of visits, the visitor is already engrossed in questioning her hosts about life in this particular town, asking what the people need and how the government can help. The period is the 1930s, and the woman is Eleanor Roosevelt.

When Franklin D. Roosevelt was elected president in 1932, his wife greeted his victory with ambivalence. After some brutally difficult years early in their marriage, Eleanor and Franklin had arrived at an understanding. From then on, they shared their five children as well as a strong commitment to social reform and to Franklin's political career, but they led relatively separate personal lives. Even after Franklin became governor of New York State in 1928, Eleanor remained independent, teaching school one day a week in New York City, writing extensively, making regular radio broadcasts, and running a crafts factory with two friends. Being the president's wife would end all that, and she feared the change would leave her with nothing to do but play hostess.

Instead, Eleanor invented a new way to be First Lady. During her White House years she spoke out regularly on public issues, often articulating positions that were considerably more liberal than her husband's current policies. She based her comments on what she learned from her vast correspondence, her huge network of personal contacts, and especially from her extensive travels around the country. Besides accompanying her husband on his occasional campaign trips, Eleanor traveled constantly on her own, often covering more than 40,000 miles a year. One typical 12-hour day in 1936 involved traveling many miles by car, giving several speeches, and visiting a school, a chicken farm, a tearoom, a craft shop, several dozen new low-cost homes, and a vacuum-cleaner assembly plant. Such trips were neither leisurely nor scenic, but because of the way that Eleanor Roosevelt looked at people and the way she listened to them, she was able to see what was unique and human in each place she visited. As a result, her travels accomplished two important things: first, she made the New Deal a vivid presence for millions of people; second,

"The one great danger for a man in public life or for the woman who is that man's wife, is that they may be set apart from the stream of life affecting the rest of the country. It is easy in Washington to think that Washington is the country and forget that it is a small place and only becomes important as the people who live there truly represent the other parts of the country."

Eleanor Roosevelt's last radio broadcast before her husband's inauguration, 1933.

she provided her husband with a remarkable perspective on what was happening to ordinary Americans during the Depression.

Eleanor communicated her views in six books, hundreds of magazine articles, thousands of speeches, a daily syndicated newspaper column, and her own radio show. She was also a relentless advocate behind the scenes, continually pointing out to her husband and the members of his administration where specific programs were falling short of their objectives, particularly in the way they served women and minorities. New Dealer Rexford Tugwell later observed: "No one who ever saw Eleanor Roosevelt sit down facing her husband, holding his eyes firmly and saying to him, 'Franklin, I think you should' . . . 'Franklin, surely you will not'. . . will ever forget the experience. . . . It would be impossible to say how often and to what extent American governmental processes have been turned in a new direction because of her determination." Understanding the importance of her contribution, Franklin supported her public and private activism even when it caused political difficulties for him.

Eleanor never entirely made her peace with the role of First Lady. She hated the lack of privacy, the numerous ceremonial duties, and the feeling—which intensified as the 1930s turned into the 1940s—that the struggle for social justice to which she dedicated her life was only one of many considerations for her husband. But if she sometimes felt discouraged, she never diminished her efforts. Starting during the Depression and continuing thereafter, Eleanor Roosevelt established a record for moral courage, effectiveness, and independence that has been equaled by no other First Lady before or since.

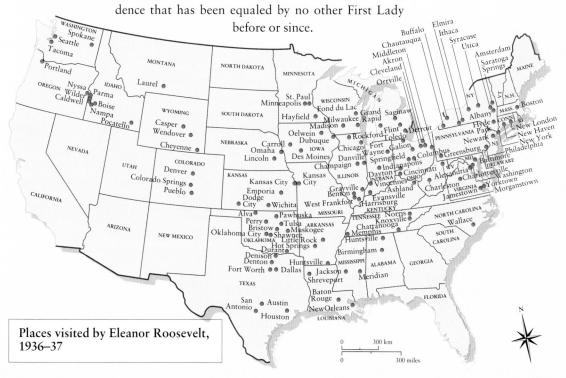

Places visited by Eleanor Roosevelt, 1936–37

World War II: Women in the Military

Women accounted for about 3 percent of all military personnel in World War II, a proportion only a few points higher than in World War I. But the *number* of women who served in World War II—nearly 400,000—was more than 10 times greater. Furthermore, many more women served overseas and they performed many more varied tasks.

The Women's Auxiliary Army Corps (WAAC), founded in May 1942, had the largest female enlistment and sent women to every theater of the war. In September 1943, the WAAC became the Women's Army Corps (WAC), a formal part of the U.S. Army. The Navy opened its doors to women in July 1942 with the creation of Women Accepted for Voluntary Emergency Service (WAVES). WAVES served in many United States locations but were not allowed overseas until late 1944; even then only a few were assigned to Hawaii and Alaska.

The third-largest group was military nurses. Army nurses served in hospitals in every war zone, and more than 1,600 were decorated for "meritorious service and bravery under fire." Women in the smaller Navy Nurse Corps served mainly in the United States and the Pacific, working on air evacuation planes and hospital ships as well as in hospitals.

The Coast Guard established its own female branch, known as the SPARS, in fall 1942, and the Women's Reserve of the Marine Corps was organized a few months later. Like the WAVES, both SPARS and female Marines spent most of the war in the United States, only reaching Hawaii and Alaska during the final months of the war.

WACs, WAVES, SPARS, and female Marines filled a broad variety of jobs, including clerical worker, radar specialist, laboratory assistant, medical technician, airplane and auto mechanic, telephone operator, translator, chauffeur,

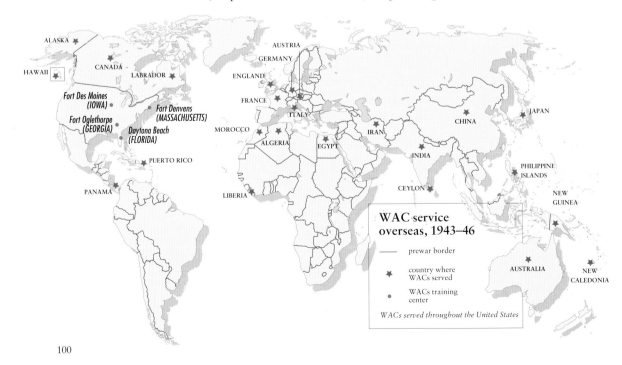

WAC service overseas, 1943–46

— prewar border

★ country where WACs served

● WACs training center

WACs served throughout the United States

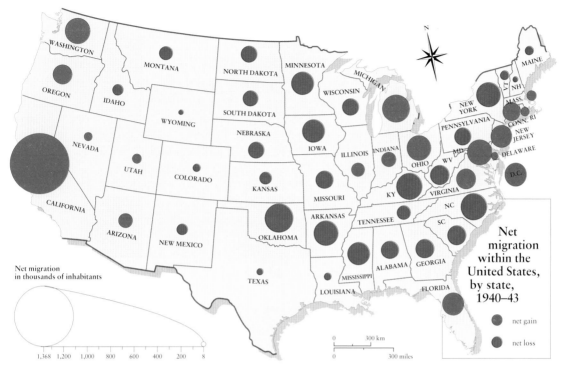

Net migration
in thousands of inhabitants

1,368 1,200 1,000 800 600 400 200 8

Net migration within the United States, by state, 1940–43

net gain

net loss

0   300 km

0   300 miles

radio intelligence officer, aerial gunnery instructor, photographer, machinist mate, air traffic controller, and parachute rigger. Especially pioneering work was done by the Women's Airforce Service Pilots (WASP), formed by the Army Air Force in July 1943 out of two earlier programs. More than 900 women served as WASPs, ferrying more than 12,000 airplanes, towing targets and gliders, providing flight instruction, and flying practice missions to train bomber crews. Yet the WASPs remained officially civilians, ineligible for military benefits or even meals in the officers' mess. Furthermore, they were the victims of continuous and inaccurate public criticism arising at least in part from the fact that many male pilots saw them as a threat. A bill to make the service an official part of the Air Force was defeated in 1944, and shortly thereafter the WASPs were disbanded.

In addition to gender discrimination, which cropped up in all the services, racial discrimination pervaded women's wartime experience. In the WACs and the Army Nurse Corps, black women had to sleep, eat, and sometimes work in segregated locations. They were entirely excluded from the WASPs and Marines, and were only admitted to the WAVES, SPARS, and Navy Nurse Corps in tiny numbers very late in the war.

Women in the military, World War II

service	approximate strength, summer 1945
Women's Army Corps (WACs)	100,000
WAVES (U.S. Navy)	92,000
Army Nurse Corps	57,000
U.S. Marine Corps Women's Reserve	20,000
Navy Nurse Corps	11,000
SPARS (U.S. Coast Guard)	11,000
Women's Airforce Service Pilots (WASPs)	1,000

In all, nearly 400,000 women served in the U.S. military during World War II

World War II: Women on the Home Front

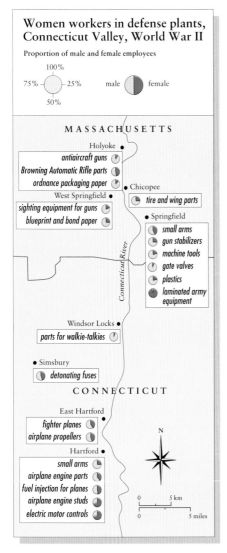

Women workers in defense plants, Connecticut Valley, World War II

Proportion of male and female employees

100%
75% — 25%   male   female
50%

MASSACHUSETTS

Holyoke
antiaircraft guns
Browning Automatic Rifle parts
ordnance packaging paper
Chicopee
West Springfield
tire and wing parts
sighting equipment for guns
blueprint and bond paper
Springfield
small arms
gun stabilizers
machine tools
gate valves
plastics
laminated army equipment

Connecticut River

Windsor Locks
parts for walkie-talkies

Simsbury
detonating fuses

CONNECTICUT

East Hartford
fighter planes
airplane propellers

N

Hartford
small arms
airplane engine parts
fuel injection for planes
airplane engine studs
electric motor controls

0   5 km
0   5 miles

Women's labor force participation, by age, 1940–50

contribution of women in each age group to the total (male and female) workforce, in percent

30
55 years and over   65 years and over
45–64 years
20
25–54 years   25–44 years
10
16–24 years   20–24 years
16–19 years
0
1940   1945   1950
years

Women who served in the military during World War II shared a certain base of common experience, whatever the inequities of military life. But on the home front, women's wartime experiences were remarkably diverse. On any given night, a Missouri housewife might be counting sugar coupons, while a defense worker in Detroit clocked in for her job as a welder, and a movie star danced with young officers at the Hollywood Canteen.

As defense workers, as wives of workers, and as service wives, women participated in the huge population shifts that took place during World War II; California alone received a net increase of nearly 1.4 million people, while Michigan added 280,000 new residents. One effect of these population surges was that thousands of women had to face not only the usual shortages and worries of wartime homemaking but also the demands of keeping house in makeshift, often acutely overcrowded quarters.

Perhaps no group of women experienced more upheaval during the war years than the Japanese Americans of California. In the panicky months following Japan's attack on Pearl Harbor in December 1941, the federal government ordered that all Japanese Americans leave the West Coast. When neighboring states refused to accept the 110,000 refugees (two thirds of whom were American-born), 10 internment camps were built for them in isolated parts of the West. Surrounded by barbed wire and armed guards, the typical camp held 10,000 people housed in bleak rows of barracks divided into cubicles, one per family. For nearly three years, Japanese women struggled to sustain their families amidst the pervasive grit of the desert, the extremes of heat and cold, the lack of privacy, the monotony of camp life, and the bitterness of imprisonment.

While the war brought exile to these women, it opened new occupational horizons for many others. About 20 million women held jobs during WWII, including nearly 7 million who had never worked before. Neither private employers nor the government did much to accommodate working women's particular problems, such as the need for child care. Nevertheless, wives joined the labor force in such large numbers that by 1945, for the first time in American history, married workers outnumbered single ones, and those over 35 outnumbered younger women.

Initially most female defense workers were assigned to

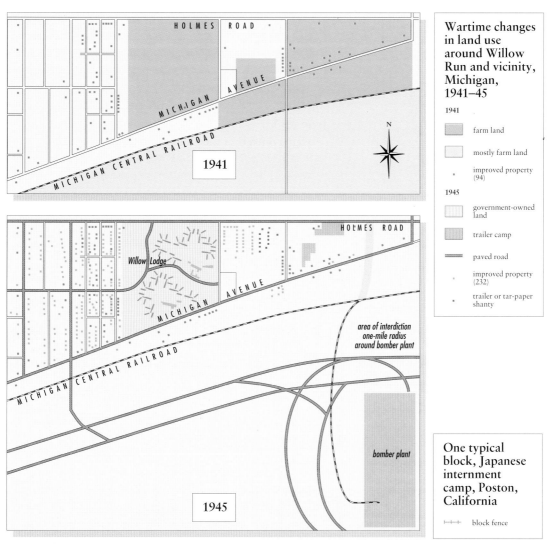

Wartime changes in land use around Willow Run and vicinity, Michigan, 1941–45

1941
- farm land
- mostly farm land
- improved property (94)

1945
- government-owned land
- trailer camp
- paved road
- improved property (232)
- trailer or tar-paper shanty

area of interdiction one-mile radius around bomber plant

bomber plant

One typical block, Japanese internment camp, Poston, California

- block fence

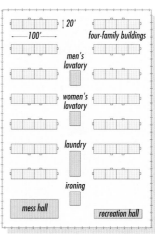

100' / 20' / four-family buildings / men's lavatory / women's lavatory / laundry / ironing / mess hall / recreation hall

clerical tasks, but by 1943 production demands forced employers to open many industrial occupations to women. In Baltimore, for instance, manufacturing jobs rose from 20 percent of female employment in 1940 to 48 percent in 1944. Even though women's wages in manufacturing averaged only 65 percent of what men were paid, these jobs still provided more money, more diverse opportunities, and better benefits than practically any traditional female jobs. At least 400,000 black women were among those who jumped at their first chance to do industrial work. Black women encountered considerable racial discrimination, but opportunities improved as labor needs increased, and even the poorest industrial jobs were generally better than the domestic or agricultural labor to which these women had been confined in the past.

The Move to the Suburbs

As World War II drew to a close, women who had only recently been encouraged to help their country by going to work were told that the health of society depended on their staying home and devoting themselves to their families. A 1945 poll showed that only 18 percent of those surveyed approved of married women working. With the advent of the Cold War the stakes grew even higher, as dedicating oneself to one's family came to be identified with preserving the American way of life.

Between 1947 and 1965, the proportion of married women who had jobs rose from 21 to 36 percent. Nevertheless, the "typical" American wife portrayed in ads, movies, novels, advice books, magazines, and newspapers during these years was a full-time housewife whose life revolved entirely around her husband and several children. The idealized setting for that life was a brand-new single-family suburban home, complete with family room, eat-in kitchen, a TV set, a wealth of electrical appliances, and a spacious backyard.

These stereotypes had some basis in reality. After years of decline, the national birthrate rebounded during the postwar years, peaking in 1957 at a level that had not been seen since 1916. Moreover, much of the fabled "baby boom" did take place in suburbia. If most new homes did not quite resemble the pictures in the magazines, it was still true that millions of young couples did start building families in the suburbs during these years, generously supported by federal dollars poured into new highways, energy policy that kept gasoline prices low, the GI Bill and FHA mortgage insurance, and national tax laws that subsidized home ownership.

The growth of the suburbs also overlapped with another important demographic change: a huge migration among people of color. Agricultural employment in the South dropped

Central city population as proportion of total metropolitan area: changes, 1940–70

1940
1970

Pittsburgh
Boston
St. Louis
Dallas
Los Angeles
Philadelphia
New York
San Francisco
Detroit
Washington
Cleveland
Houston
Chicago
Baltimore
Minneapolis-St. Paul

0 10 20 30 40 50 60 70 80

Central Business District as proportion of
Standard Metropolitan Statistical Area population, in percent

sharply after the introduction of the mechanical cotton picker, while northern industry was booming, especially during the war. In response, about 5 million African Americans left the South for cities up north or in the Far West between 1940 and 1960. They were joined by several million immigrants from Latin America—especially Puerto Ricans in New York City and Mexicans in California. These black and Hispanic newcomers did not join the postwar move to the suburbs, however. Instead, racial, ethnic, and class discrimination kept most of them confined to overcrowded urban slums. Over time, as the suburbs began to draw jobs and stores as well as residents from the cities, many African-American and Latina women would find themselves marooned in city neighborhoods that offered few services, declining employment, and a troubling outlook for their children's future.

These trends were not widely recognized during the 1950s, but there was growing discussion about whether those women who did get to live in the suburbs benefited from that life. Critics deplored the narrow horizons and enforced self-sacrifice of suburban homemaking, while supporters insisted that devoting oneself to marriage and motherhood represented women's surest path to fulfillment. Meanwhile, the fact that millions of American women were socially or financially excluded from being "typical" suburban housewives would not receive serious public attention until the 1960s.

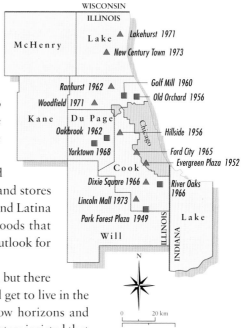

Regional shopping centers, Chicago area, 1949–73

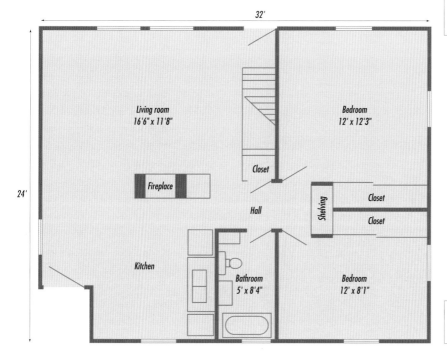

Levittown ranchhouse, 1949

Confronting the Question of Race

The modern Civil Rights Movement can be said to have begun in 1955 in Montgomery, Alabama, when a woman—Rosa Parks—refused to give up her bus seat to a white passenger. Throughout the next decade, as protesters defied segregation throughout the South, women participated every step of the way. In fact, one of the final events in the movement's most vibrant 10 years as a bi-racial campaign for integration was the murder of a woman, Viola Liuzzo, just after the Selma to Montgomery march in 1965.

The story of the Montgomery bus boycott illuminates women's importance to the movement. As soon as Parks' arrest sparked the decision to mount a boy-cott, Jo Ann Robinson, an English professor at Alabama State College, orga-nized the writing of a leaflet to announce the plan and had it mimeographed and distributed throughout the city over the weekend. That Monday, hardly a black passenger was to be seen on a city bus. For the next eleven months, until the protesters won their case in the U.S. Supreme Court, black female domestic workers made a particularly heavy sacrifice for the boycott because many had to travel long distances to their jobs in the white suburbs. Yet these women held their ground, getting rides when they could and walking miles when they had to. Interviewed during the boycott, one woman gave the entire movement a message to live by: "My feet are weary," she said, "but my soul is rested."

Fot the next 10 years, women participated in every sit-in, every march, and every Freedom Ride. Southern blacks took the lead, but many northern college students also participated, as did performers such as Mary Travers, Joan Baez, Odetta, and Judy Collins. Meanwhile, older women across the South (many black, some white) donated money, joined local marches, turned out for voter registration, and provided the young activists with food and shelter.

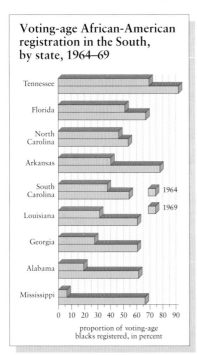

Voting-age African-American registration in the South, by state, 1964–69

Tennessee

Florida

North Carolina

Arkansas

South Carolina

Louisiana

Georgia

Alabama

Mississippi

1964
1969

0 10 20 30 40 50 60 70 80 90

proportion of voting-age
blacks registered, in percent

Yet the movement contained a troubling paradox: Its com-mitment to equality did not always include equality between genders. In the "freedom houses" where the young activists lived, women did the cooking and cleaning. At movement offices, women typed and filed; men made the public state-ments. Women offered suggestions; men made policy. Sexual relations complicated matters further. If a woman refused to have sex with a fellow activist she might be called frigid or (depending on the man involved) racist; if she agreed, she might be taken less seriously as a colleague. It is a measure of how complicated gender relations became that when two movement stalwarts, Casey Hayden and Mary King, wrote a paper on the position of women for a meeting of the Student Non-Violent Coordinating Committee in 1964, they did so anonymously. Their fears were no doubt confirmed when the president, Stokely Carmichael, responded: "The only position for women in SNCC is prone." The experiences of women in the Civil Rights Movement—both positive and negative—helped pave the way for the birth of modern feminism.

1. **1955 Montgomery, AL:** Rosa Parks is arrested for refusing to move to the back of a city bus. The resulting boycott brings national attention to the Civil Rights Movement.

2. **1956 Tuscaloosa, AL:** Autherine Lucy becomes the first black to attend a class at the University of Alabama.

3. **1957 Atlanta, GA:** Executive director Ella Baker sets up the headquarters of the new Southern Christian Leadership Conference.

4. **1957 Little Rock, AK:** The first black students at Central High School, the Little Rock Nine, including six girls, endure months of threats and abuse.

5. **1957–61 New Market, TN:** At the Highlander Research and Education Center, which she runs with her husband, Zilphia Horton writes new words to an old union song and publishes it as "We Shall Overcome."

6. **1957 Johns Island, SC:** Bernice Robinson, a beautician, directs one of the movement's earliest citizenship schools; her program is later used in many other rural communities.

7. **1960 Nashville, TN:** Student leader Diane Nash confronts the mayor publicly, asking if he supports their goal. His assent sets the stage for the first desegregation agreement in a southern city.

8. **1960 Raleigh, NC:** Ella Baker arranges the first large meeting of young civil rights protesters. At her urging, they form their own organization: the Student Non-violent Coordinating Committee.

9. **1961 Rock Hill, SC:** Pioneering SNCC's "jail, no bail" strategy, Ruby Doris Smith spends a full month in jail, becoming one of the first civil rights protesters to serve out a full sentence.

10. **1961 Athens, GA:** Charlayne Hunter is one of two students who integrate the University of Georgia despite harassment and mob threats.

11. **1961–65 Midway, GA:** At Dorchester Academy, Septima Clark directs a center for citizenship training, voter registration, and leadership retreats, serving movement participants from all over the South.

12. **1963 Greenwood, MS:** Endesha Idea Mae Holland, a churchgoer and civil rights activist who was formerly a prostitute, joins a local minister in leading Greenwood's first mass march.

13. **1963 Birmingham, AL:** When a bomb explodes in the 16th Street Baptist Church, four black girls aged 11 to 14 are killed. They are Denise McNair, Addie Mae Collins, Carole Robertson, and Cynthia Wesley.

14. **1963 Jackson, MS:** Pearlena Lewis, Anne Moody, and a male fellow student from Tougaloo University are assaulted when they try to integrate the lunch counter at the local Woolworth's.
    Clarie Collins Harvey organizes Womanpower Unlimited to provide civil rights workers with food, shelter, and help in contacting their families.

15. **1963 Selma, AL:** Despite ongoing surveillance and bomb threats, Amelia Boynton and her husband, longtime local activists, make their home a safe house for SNCC workers.

16. **1964 Palmer's Crossing, MS:** Victoria Gray organizes citizenship classes for adults in local homes and churches, stressing literacy and voter registration as the keys to integration.

17. **1964 Waveland, MS:** At an SNCC staff retreat, Casey Hayden and Mary King submit an anonymous paper on the subordinated position of women in the Civil Rights Movement.

18. **1964 McComb, MS:** When Alyene Quin becomes active in the McComb movement, her café is closed down by the police and her home is bombed.

19. **1964 Jackson, MS:** Fannie Lou Hamer, Annie Devine, and Victoria Gray are among those chosen to lead the Mississippi Freedom Democrat Party delegation in a challenge to the state's all-white representatives at the Democratic Convention.

20. **1965 Lowndesboro, AL:** Viola Liuzzo, a white housewife from Detroit, is shot and killed by Klansmen while she is driving participants back from the Selma to Montgomery March.

1940

1960

1980

Black neighborhoods in Philadelphia, 1940–80

over 40% black

Women in the Civil Rights Movement, 1955–65

PART V: REDEFINING WOMEN'S PLACE: 1965 TO THE PRESENT

Soon after President John F. Kennedy took office in 1961, his only female senior official, Esther Peterson, persuaded him to establish a President's Commission on the Status of Women. The commission's report, *American Women* (1963), revealed the following: Women's wages had actually declined compared to men's during the previous decade; wives had little claim on the assets they helped their husbands acquire; they held few elective offices; women were notably underrepresented in the upper levels of government, business, and most professions; and neither the government nor private industry made much provision for services that were crucial for working women, such as maternity leave and child care. All this, despite the fact that women represented half the population, had been voting for more than 40 years, and now constituted one out of every three American workers.

Between the mid-1960s and the end of the twentieth century, the place of women in American society changed significantly, particularly when contrasted with the relative lack of change over the previous 50 years. How did this happen?

The first answer is what women did for themselves. While the report of the president's commission helped awaken policy makers to the fact of gender discrimination, the mass of American women were reached on a more visceral level by the appearance that same year of Betty Friedan's *The Feminine Mystique*. Friedan drew on insights that had been simmering for years, but she articulated them with a verve and passion that turned long-standing concerns into a national movement.

Friedan's book came at an opportune time. Many young women had participated in the Civil Rights Movement, the student movement, and the protests against the Vietnam War. On the one hand, these crusades provided a compelling model of how to effect social change. On the other hand, the persistent sexism displayed by male activists in these movements led many female participants to start thinking about their own right to equal treatment. As for older feminists, many of them had come of age in the labor movement, where they too had experienced the excitement of mass organizing and the bitterness of gender discrimination.

Inspired by Friedan's book and their own histories, the feminist leaders promoted the cause of female equality through dozens of new organizations, exuberant marches and protests, political lobbying, and a series of groundbreaking lawsuits. Meanwhile, millions of less visible women brought the struggle closer to home, organizing their own "consciousness-raising" sessions and confronting the men in their lives with new questions about such familiar transactions as who made the coffee at work and who did the dishes at home.

Within a decade, the national enthusiasm for social reforms of all kinds cooled, a victim of white backlash against the gains made by African Americans, of African Americans' own frustration that the reforms had not gone further, the Vietnam War, President Richard Nixon's near-impeachment, and a weaker national economy. The election of Ronald Reagan to the presidency in 1980 confirmed the trend toward more conservative policies. In terms of women's issues, this trend was reflected in the failure of the Equal Rights Amendment, cutbacks in many government programs for poor families, the emergence of a new "antifeminist" movement, and growing restrictions on the right to abortion (as granted by the Supreme Court in *Roe v. Wade*, 1973).

Given these changes, it seemed possible that the 1980s and 1990s would bring the same reaffirmation of traditional gender roles that occurred in the United States after each world war. But that did not happen. Women continued to gain ground during the final decades of the twentieth century, thanks both to their own persistence and to the ongoing economic and social changes in American life. Starting in the mid-1970s, men's wages declined so significantly that most wives had to go to work just to meet expenses. The same years also saw a significant increase in the number of women heading their own households. Both trends led more women to enter the labor force. In fact, by the end of the twentieth century the rate of employment among married women was about the same as that among single women: 60 percent. Working mothers often found the combination of job and home responsibilities stressful, yet the economic importance of their work and the satisfaction that many derived from it made it unrealistic to expect that American women would soon return to the idealized domesticity that some antifeminists advocated.

Women's political gains during the late twentieth century are reflected in this picture of Washington State's female legislators, who in 1999 constituted 41 percent of the state legislature.

As the twentieth century drew to a close, the sexes still remained far from equal—in earning power, professional status, or political clout. Yet, despite some antipathy to the *idea* of feminism when labeled as such, the feminists' core argument—that women deserved to be taken seriously and treated equally—had profoundly influenced American society. The effects could be seen in the network of new laws prohibiting gender discrimination and sexual harassment; the frequent representation of female perspectives in the arts, humanities, and social sciences; the improved provisions for maternal leave; women's growing share of electoral offices; their rising wages in relation to men's; and their increased presence in the upper levels of business, government, and the professions.

Much work remained to be done, particularly in ensuring that the progress enjoyed by the most fortunate women was shared by all women. But a review of the final decades of the twentieth century makes clear that during those years women did manage to broaden the range of choices available to them, to make their voices heard more clearly in the national dialogue, and to win themselves a more equal place in American society.

Conflict and Dissent in the Late 1960s

As the Civil Rights Movement split along racial lines after 1965, black and white female activists moved in different directions. From time to time they would come together again over a particular issue, but the interracial "beloved community" that many had envisioned during the early civil rights years was rarely mentioned after 1965.

For black women, racial loyalties spoke loudest. Some aligned themselves with militant groups such as the Black Panthers; others expressed their frustration by joining in the urban riots that exploded during these years; others worked to create new housing, help children, or reduce poverty in African-American communities. The Black Pride movement reinforced this focus on black life rather than on integration, and it also fostered a new enthusiasm for black culture. Many black women began wearing African textiles, leaving their hair "natural" instead of straightening it, and taking new pride in their black English. As Chicano, Native American, and Asian women began asserting their own political and cultural identities, they too helped highlight the strengths and the grievances shared by America's women of color.

White women turned their attention to a variety of other causes. The campus-based New Left, launched in the early 1960s, offered a broadening critique of American society—not only its injustices but also its materialism at home and imperialism abroad. Student radicals posed some of the earliest questions about America's expanding commitment to the war in Vietnam, helping to organize the first antiwar "teach-ins" in 1965 and the first major antiwar rallies in 1967. Women joined the many marches, were clubbed by

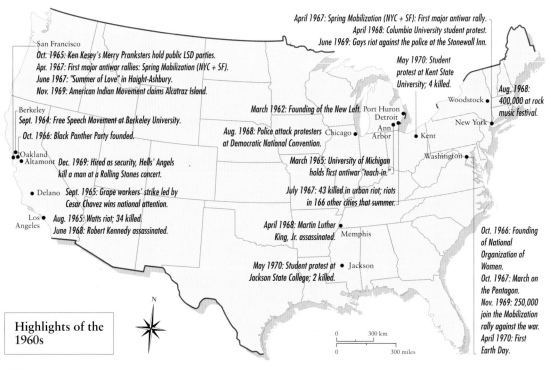

April 1967: Spring Mobilization (NYC + SF): First major antiwar rally.
April 1968: Columbia University student protest.
June 1969: Gays riot against the police at the Stonewall Inn.

San Francisco
Oct. 1965: Ken Kesey's Merry Pranksters hold public LSD parties.
Apr. 1967: First major antiwar rallies: Spring Mobilization (NYC + SF).
June 1967: "Summer of Love" in Haight-Ashbury.
Nov. 1969: American Indian Movement claims Alcatraz Island.

May 1970: Student protest at Kent State University; 4 killed.

Aug. 1968: 400,000 at rock music festival.

Woodstock

Berkeley
Sept. 1964: Free Speech Movement at Berkeley University.

Oct. 1966: Black Panther Party founded.

March 1962: Founding of the New Left. Port Huron
Detroit

New York

Oakland
Altamont Dec. 1969: Hired as security, Hells' Angels kill a man at a Rolling Stones concert.

Aug. 1968: Police attack protesters at Democratic National Convention. Chicago Ann Arbor Kent

Washington

March 1965: University of Michigan holds first antiwar "teach-in."

Delano Sept. 1965: Grape workers' strike led by Cesar Chavez wins national attention.

July 1967: 43 killed in urban riot; riots in 166 other cities that summer.

Los Angeles Aug. 1965: Watts riot; 34 killed.
June 1968: Robert Kennedy assassinated.

April 1968: Martin Luther King, Jr. assassinated. Memphis

Oct. 1966: Founding of National Organization of Women.
Oct. 1967: March on the Pentagon.
Nov. 1969: 250,000 join the Mobilization rally against the war.
April 1970: First Earth Day.

May 1970: Student protest at Jackson State College; 2 killed. Jackson

Highlights of the 1960s

N

0   300 km

0   300 miles

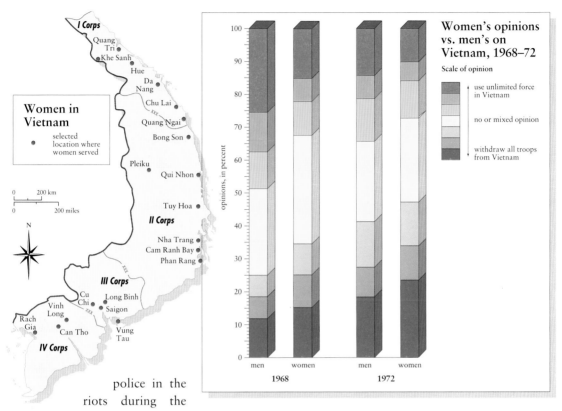

Women in Vietnam

• selected location where women served

0   200 km
0   200 miles

N

I Corps
Quang Tri
Khe Sanh
Hue
Da Nang
Chu Lai
Quang Ngai
Bong Son

Pleiku
Qui Nhon
Tuy Hoa

II Corps
Nha Trang
Cam Ranh Bay
Phan Rang

III Corps
Cu Chi
Long Binh
Vinh Long
Saigon
Rach Gia
Can Tho
Vung Tau

IV Corps

Women's opinions vs. men's on Vietnam, 1968–72

Scale of opinion

↑ use unlimited force in Vietnam

no or mixed opinion

↓ withdraw all troops from Vietnam

opinions, in percent

men   women   men   women
   1968   1972

police in the riots during the Chicago Democratic Convention in 1968, and helped close down college campuses in protest against the expansion of the war into Cambodia in 1970. Yet there were women on all sides of this question; even as some women were putting roses in soldiers' gun barrels during the March on the Pentagon, others were mourning the death of their husbands in the war, and more than 10,000 were themselves doing military service in Vietnam.

Women were also active celebrants in the cultural rebellion of the late 1960s—a sweeping rejection of middle-class proprieties that combined sexual freedom (facilitated by the newly available birth-control pill), rock music, drugs, long hair, and the maxim, "Don't trust anyone over 30." For some women, "flower power" meant life on a commune instead of a conventional life in the suburbs. For others, it simply meant rock concerts and the right "hippie" clothing. But in all its multiple meanings, the heady mix of iconoclasm and sensuality reverberated through society, reshaping American politics, fashion, music, design, speech, and social behavior.

Women were wholehearted participants in all these events and yet, as had happened in the Civil Rights Movement, they often felt that they were being treated dismissively by their male compatriots. As just one example, many felt that their role as protesters was belittled by the draft-resistance slogan: "Girls says yes to guys who say no." Experiences like these convinced a number of female activists that the time had come to affirm their own right to equality.

Confronting the Question of Gender

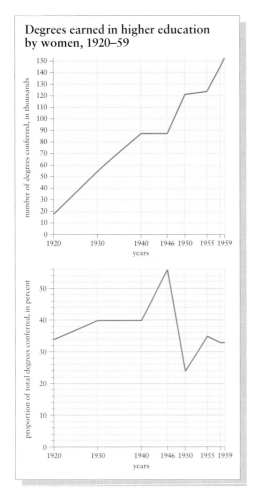

Degrees earned in higher education by women, 1920–59

Throughout the late 1960s, while different groups of women were protesting the Vietnam War or demanding Black Power, a growing number were also beginning to speak out on a subject that had remained largely quiescent for 50 years: women's rights. Nineteenth-century feminists had envisioned the vote as only one aspect of full equality, but the drive for woman suffrage had gradually overshadowed all other goals. Once that victory was won in 1920, the rest of the agenda was forgotten; indeed, the flappers of the 1920s saw their mothers' feminism as a bit old-fashioned. In the decades that followed, different groups of women did periodically demand greater equality, but these protests never coalesced into a single unified women's movement.

Modern feminism burst into public consciousness with the appearance of Betty Friedan's book, *The Feminine Mystique*, in 1963. Friedan maintained that a life devoted exclusively to husband and children left many women feeling empty and unfulfilled. These women had no language to express their feelings, yet millions of them, said Friedan, were suffering from "the problem that has no name." A few months thereafter, the report of the President's Commission on the Status of Women appeared, documenting in more concrete ways the problems that women faced.

The available data made clear that women had plenty of reason to complain; they continued to earn significantly less than men and they were underrepresented in every important profession, in business management, in senior academic posts, and in the upper levels of government. Yet neither the commission report nor the Civil

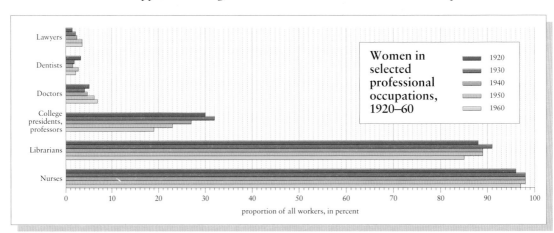

Women in selected professional occupations, 1920–60

1920
1930
1940
1950
1960

Rights Act of 1964 (which included a prohibition against sexual discrimination) appeared to inspire systematic government action. Accordingly, in 1966 Friedan and her allies founded the National Organization for Women, dedicated to pursuing equal rights by means of legislative lobbying and legal test cases. NOW's agenda was soon taken much further by radical feminists, who attacked the whole system of gender relations, including everything from job discrimination to abortion rights. Across the country, these women began marching, picketing, and organizing "consciousness-raising sessions" to share their experiences and articulate their grievances.

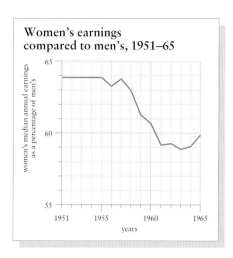

Developing a unified women's movement continued to be difficult. While feminists struggled among themselves to define their positions on issues ranging from marriage to politics to the role of lesbians in the movement, many working women (particularly African Americans and Latinas) dismissed the whole struggle as too focused on the woes of privileged suburbanites. Meanwhile, many housewives took the feminist critique of domesticity as an attack on their own life choices.

These attitudes helped shape the fortunes of the Equal Rights Amendment, which was feared by many women as a threat to legal protections they valued, such as alimony, child support, and exemption from the draft. Vilified in a passionate Stop ERA campaign featuring conservative Phyllis Schlafly, the amendment never achieved ratification. Yet despite many setbacks, the fundamental idea that women deserved an equal place in American society continued to make gradual headway, reflected not only in legislation and social practice, but even in the assertive rhetoric and busy public lives of the movement's most vociferous female opponents.

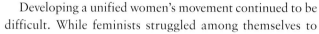

Recent Trends in Women's Work

Occupations with more than 90 percent female employees, 1996

Dental assistants	99.1%
Dental hygienists	98.2%
Kindergarten and prekindergarten teachers	98.1%
Secretaries, stenos, and typists	97.8%
Private household child-care workers	97.1%
Receptionists	96.9%
Early childhood teachers' assistants	95.4%
Licensed practical nurses	95.3%
Registered nurses	93.3%
Speech therapists	93.3%
Teachers' aides	92.1%
Bookkeepers, accounting, and auditing clerks	91.9%
Hairdressers and cosmetologists	91.1%
Payroll and time-keeping clerks	90.7%
Telephone operators	90.5%
Statistical clerks	90.3%
Bank tellers	90.1%

Three important patterns characterized the world of women's work at the end of the twentieth century: first, many more women held jobs than in the past; second, women worked in a much greater variety of occupations; and third, despite the new opportunities, most women continued to hold the kinds of jobs traditionally associated with female employment.

Single women had always been active in the workforce, but between 1960 and 1995 the proportion of married women with jobs doubled. Even greater was the change among married women with children under the age of six; their participation rate climbed from 19 to 64 percent. Many factors contributed to these changes, including women's own rising aspirations, affirmative action laws that encouraged female hiring, and some increase in supportive arrangements such as day care and flexible scheduling. Perhaps the greatest influence was the steady decline in the value of men's wages after 1973, which made it increasingly difficult for families to live on one income. A generation earlier, married women seldom worked unless they were poor or unusually career-minded. By the end of the twentieth century, the two-income family had become the norm.

The final decades of the twentieth century brought a dramatic opening up of occupational choices. By the 1990s, women had established a strong presence in professions such as architecture, medicine, and the law, and they accounted for nearly half the workforce in such traditionally male fields as public administration, financial management, journalism, and biological research. Nevertheless, they continued to be underrepresented in virtually all the best-paid, highest-status positions within each field. Some women themselves chose less-demanding jobs that combined better with their responsibilities for home and child-rearing; female doctors, for instance, tended to cluster

Female labor force participation, by state, 1995

Proportion of women over 15 employed or looking for work, in percent

69.6
65.0
61.3
60.0
57.0
46.3

Occupation by gender, 1995

proportion of workers aged over 15, in percent

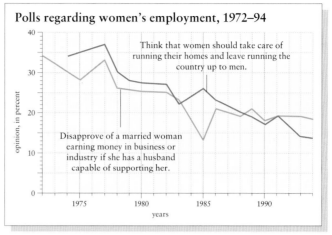

Polls regarding women's employment, 1972–94

Think that women should take care of running their homes and leave running the country up to men.

Disapprove of a married woman earning money in business or industry if she has a husband capable of supporting her.

in specialties that involved fewer years of training and more predictable work schedules. But personal preference alone does not explain the pattern of female employment. Even very ambitious and talented women were sometimes passed over for top positions because of doubts about their capacity or commitment. Such women, it was sometimes said, had hit the "glass ceiling"—the point beyond which the men in charge were not comfortable with female advancement. Thus, even though there were many new occupational choices available, women's careers continued to be affected by their disproportionate responsibility for child-rearing and by lingering patterns of gender discrimination.

The majority of women continued to work in the kinds of occupations long associated with female employment—jobs such as dental assistant, kindergarten teacher, secretary, receptionist, and nurse. Besides facing their own obstacles to advancement, these women often confronted more concrete problems, such as poor working conditions, low wages and benefits, and the growing danger of layoffs. In addition, they had to deal with two problems that were familiar to working women at every occupational level: sexual harassment in the workplace, and the persistent "double shift"—the expectation that women should spend their days doing their paid jobs and their nights and weekends doing the family housekeeping.

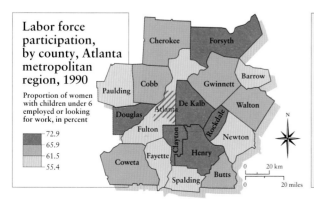

Labor force participation, by county, Atlanta metropolitan region, 1990

Proportion of women with children under 6 employed or looking for work, in percent

72.9
65.9
61.5
55.4

Working mothers in the eight wealthiest counties of the Atlanta metropolitan area, 1990

counties	median income, in $	percent of mothers in the workforce with children under 6
Fayette	53,845	55.4
Cobb	48,415	62.0
Gwinnett	48,000	64.8
Rockdale	42,838	66.3
Cherokee	41,672	64.1
De Kalb	41,495	72.9
Henry	40,733	66.9
Forsyth	40,718	65.9

115

Recent Trends in Women's Income

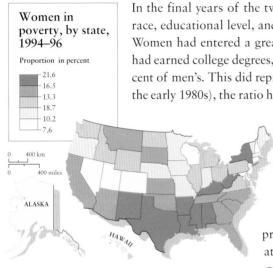

Women in poverty, by state, 1994–96

Proportion in percent

- 21.6
- 16.5
- 13.3
- 18.7
- 10.2
- 7.6

0   400 km

0   400 miles

ALASKA

HAWAII

Female-headed households in poverty, Ohio, by county, 1990

Proportion in percent

- 58.0
- 41.0
- 34.5
- 30.5
- 24.8
- 11.9

Toledo

Cleveland

Youngstown

Akron

Finlay

Canton

Springfield

Columbus

Dayton

Chilicothe

Cincinnati

N

0   500 km

0   500 miles

In the final years of the twentieth century, within virtually every age group, race, educational level, and social class women earned less money than men. Women had entered a great variety of new occupational fields and millions had earned college degrees, yet in 1996 their earnings still averaged only 74 percent of men's. This did represent progress; for nearly 25 years (from 1959 until the early 1980s), the ratio had been stuck at about 60 percent. Nevertheless, the "gender gap" remained.

One reason for women's lower income was the fact that so many of them worked in poorly paid occupations, such as clerical work and service jobs. But the gender gap could be found even within specific occupations. From investment banking to carpentry, the tradition of preferring males for supervisory positions perpetuated income disparity between the sexes. So did men's greater seniority, their higher rates of union membership, and their wider access to the informal networks that lead to raises and promotions. Moreover, at the upper end of the scale, many male executives had wives who devoted their lives to supporting their husbands' careers, freeing them from virtually all nonwork responsibilities. Few husbands were willing to play a similar role.

Women's child-rearing responsibilities were a significant factor in their lower earnings. When because of their children women entered the workforce later or took a few years off in mid-career, or chose part-time jobs, or avoided positions that involved extended travel or long hours, these decisions usually cost them money, both in lost raises and in the lost opportunity to keep pace with their male colleagues. Most women considered the rewards of parenting worth the sacrifice, yet many also noted that few husbands felt obliged to make a similar commitment to their children.

The disparity between male and female earnings often caused a sharp drop in a woman's standard of living after a divorce, giving force to feminist Gloria Steinem's observation that every married woman is just one man away from welfare. Women on their own—whether divorced or unmarried—faced particular difficulties if there were children to care for and the fathers did not contribute their share of the cost. Single mothers in their teens also found it hard to complete the education they needed to earn an adequate living in the future.

Statistics on what has been called the "feminization of poverty" help to illuminate the difficulties created by women's lower earning power combined with their role as primary parent. In 1997, among the

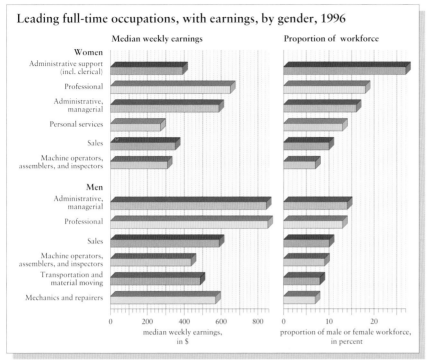

growing number of families composed of women raising children on their own, more than 40 percent had incomes below the poverty line; the rate was even higher among blacks and Latinas. For 60 years, the national welfare program ensured that families in such circumstances would receive a minimal level of support. The phasing out of this program, starting in 1995, provided some women with new opportunities, but the federal oversight role was virtually eliminated, and few states initiated systematic follow-up to ensure that every woman removed from welfare found work that would sustain her and her children.

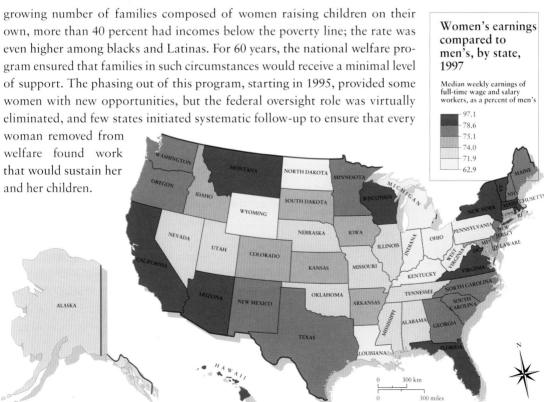

Recent Trends in Women's Immigration

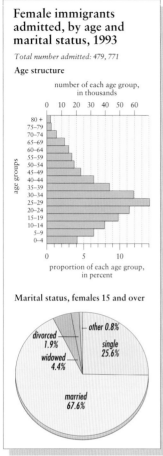

Female immigrants admitted, by age and marital status, 1993

Total number admitted: 479, 771

Age structure

number of each age group, in thousands

age groups

proportion of each age group, in percent

Marital status, females 15 and over

- other 0.8%
- single 25.6%
- divorced 1.9%
- widowed 4.4%
- married 67.6%

During the final decades of the twentieth century, immigration into the United States soared to unprecedented heights. The majority of these newcomers were women and most of them came from Asia, the Caribbean, Mexico, and Central and South America.

Men had dominated the last great surge of immigration at the beginning of the century. During those years, virtually all Asian women were excluded. And even in ethnic groups that faced no formal restrictions, female immigrants tended to be outnumbered by the many men who made the trip on their own. Relatively few foreigners arrived during the 1920s and 1930s, thanks to the restrictive legislation passed in 1924 and the economic crisis of the Great Depression. But World War II and the Cold War brought a new wave of female immigrants because so many American men went overseas as soldiers, diplomats, or businessmen and came home with foreign brides.

Female immigration was further encouraged by the Immigration and Nationality Act of 1965, which ended the former national quota system and made family reunification a primary reason for admission. Throughout the second half of the century, women represented more than half of all immigrants (54 percent in 1996), the great majority coming in as family members of citizens or resident aliens. Women clearly valued this opportunity, but it also made them highly dependent on the relatives (usually men) who vouched for them; some women endured deprivation and even abuse for fear that speaking out against their sponsors might endanger their immigration status.

The immigration quotas that had been in force between 1924 to 1965 heavily favored northern Europeans. However, residents of the Western Hemisphere were admitted

Foreign-born population, by state, 1990

Proportion of foreign-born in total population in percent

- 21.7
- 8.6
- 4.0
- 2.6
- 1.7
- 0.8

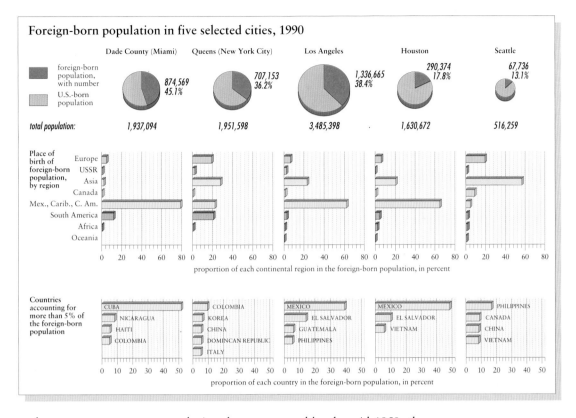

Foreign-born population in five selected cities, 1990

under a separate arrangement during these years, and by the mid-1950s they had begun arriving in large numbers. Then the 1965 immigration law, followed by the Vietnam War, opened the door to millions of Asians as well. Overall, between 1960 and 1996 while people from the Americas held steady at 44 percent of all immigrants, Europeans dropped from 45 percent to 16, and Asians soared from 8 percent to 34.

Female immigrants worked hard in their new country, often taking jobs that native-born women avoided—in domestic service, hospitals, hotels, and sweatshops. Nevertheless, some Americans began to suggest that the country had reached a point of "overload." Immigration had increased sharply, reaching an all-time high of 1.8 million in 1991, and its impact was more visible because a few parts of the country—notably New York, California, Texas, and Florida—received a disproportionate share of the newcomers, as well as a large share of the country's estimated 5 million undocumented aliens. Moreover, the fact that most new immigrants were people of color did little to make them more welcome. A number of laws were passed limiting their access to public services. Nevertheless, given the pervasive poverty in most Third World countries and the limited opportunities for women there, female immigrants continued to arrive, counting—like so many millions before them—on their capacity to make the American dream come true.

Occupations in which new female immigrants were overrepresented, 1990

	as proportion of all employed women
Sewing machine operators	73%
Dressmakers	55%
Farm workers	51%
Maids	49%
Laundering machine operators	49%
Graders and sorters	49%
Packaging machine operators	48%
Pressing machine operators	47%
Electrical equipment assemblers	45%
Other machine operators	45%

Recent Trends in Women and Politics

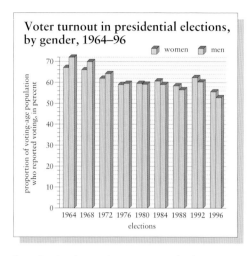

Voter turnout in presidential elections, by gender, 1964–96

During the final decades of the twentieth century, women became increasingly visible in the political life of the country. For much of the century, men had been more regular voters than women, but starting in the 1960s, male turnout rates began to decline. (Women's fell, too, but more slowly.) The effect was that by 1980, women were voting more consistently than men. This fact, combined with the larger number of females in the voting-age population, meant that women were now in a position to decide a national election if enough of them voted the same way.

The power of female voters over male was not tested for many years, since both genders usually gave their majority votes to the same candidates. Nevertheless, in nearly every presidential election from 1972 on, a greater proportion of women than men voted Democratic. By 1996 this trend combined with women's growing majority in the electorate to make history. That year, female voters turned out in such numbers for Democrat William Clinton that they carried the election, offsetting men's Republican and third-party votes. Meanwhile, at the state level in 1994 and 1996 female Democratic votes provided the margin of victory in 14 Senate races and three gubernatorial campaigns.

Over the course of American history, a number of women had offered themselves as presidential candidates, including Victoria Woodhull (1872), Belva Bennett Lockwood (1884, 1888),

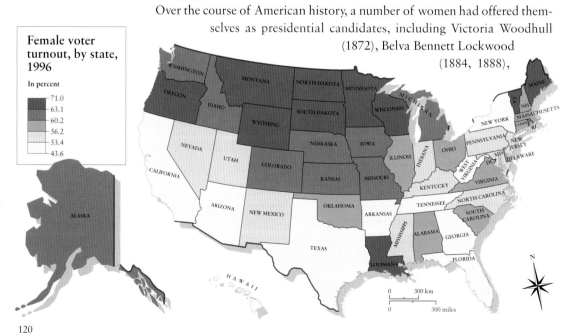

Female voter turnout, by state, 1996

In percent

71.0
63.1
60.2
56.2
53.4
43.6

0   300 km

0   300 miles

Margaret Chase Smith (1964), Shirley Chisholm (1972), and Patricia Schroeder (1988), but the only woman to receive a major-party nomination was Democrat Geraldine Ferraro, who ran unsuccessfully for vice president in 1984. More progress was made at other levels of government. By 1998, 63 women, including

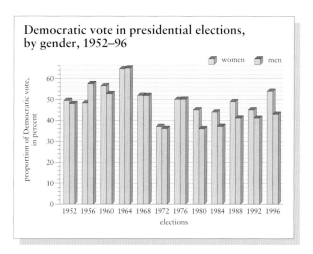

Democratic vote in presidential elections, by gender, 1952–96

19 women of color, were serving in the U.S. Congress—10 percent of the total, up from 5 percent in 1986. Women did even better in state government, where there were 1,652 female legislators—22 percent of the total; this rate, too, had doubled in a decade.

What explains this progress, particularly in an era when feminism was often described as being on the defensive? One factor was the female backlash after the confirmation of Supreme Court nominee Clarence Thomas in 1991. When the Senate chose to confirm Thomas despite Professor Anita Hill's claim that he had sexually harassed her while acting as her supervisor, it confirmed many women's belief that men held disproportionate power in the workplace and in government. Two other factors in women's electoral success were the growing pool of women with experience in the lower ranks of political office, and the success of fund-raising groups such as Emily's List and the Women's Campaign

Fund, which gave targeted support to many female candidates.

In 1776, Abigail Adams urged her husband to "remember the ladies" when the Continental Congress drafted its plans for the new republic. More than 200 years later, American women were coming closer to the day when the ladies would not have to be "remembered" by those in political power; the ladies would be among them.

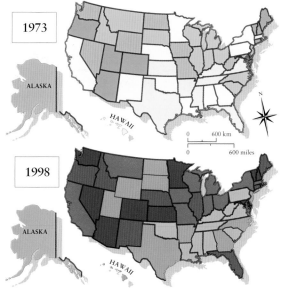

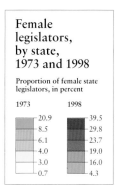

Female legislators, by state, 1973 and 1998

Proportion of female state legislators, in percent

1973	1998
20.9	39.5
8.5	29.8
6.1	23.7
4.0	19.0
3.0	16.0
0.7	4.3

Georganna Deas, Speaking Truth to Power

Seated around a conference table, the predominantly white members of the municipal hospital board are debating a proposal to turn one of the city's public hospitals over to a for-profit corporation. In the audience, more than 100 neighborhood people—many of them black or Hispanic—are urging the board to vote the proposal down. Finally, the chairwoman turns to a black board member, one of the few members who supports the community position, and says sharply: "Please tell your people to be quiet." At that, a neighborhood resident—Georganna Deas—springs to her feet, points her finger at the chairwoman, and shouts: "No! As long as you're the chair, we're *your* people!"

Georganna Deas has been rising to one occasion or another most of her life. She was only a few months old in 1948 when her parents, like many African Americans, left South Carolina for the North. Deas stayed behind in Charleston in the care of her grandmother. Then, starting when she was 11, the roles were reversed as her grandmother's failing health required the young girl to become the caretaker. The two had always been poor, with no income beyond the grandmother's wages as a domestic servant, but Deas remembers that the first time she *felt* poor was when she saw the way the charity hospital treated her grandmother. "It was almost like the Sanitation Department," she says. "Just don't die on the street."

After her grandmother died in 1965, Deas went north to Brooklyn to live with her mother, who by then was struggling to support several younger children. She finished high school, moved in briefly with her older sister, and by the age of 20 was living on her own, a single mother with a newborn son. For the next 10 years, she and her sister both scrambled to survive, arranging child care as best they could, working at whatever jobs they could find, but earning so little that periodically they were forced, as Deas recalls, to "take money from the Welfare."

The turning point came in 1979, when they saw a small newspaper ad for a program that trained women in the skilled trades. That eight-week program changed their lives. While her sister became one of the first female longshoremen on the New Jersey docks, Deas was hired as the first woman in the Bellevue Hospital Engineering Department. The commute to work took her almost two hours each way, and she had to prove herself over and over with each new group of male coworkers. But she loved the job—both the steady satisfaction of doing demanding useful work, and the special moments like the day she repaired a crucial machine in the middle of an open-heart operation. As time passed, however, Deas became increasingly aware that she would never get the same opportunities for advancement as the men around her. Finally, she says, "I was waking up angry too many days." With her pension secure, she left Bellevue after 10 years.

The jobs Deas held from then on never engaged her as Bellevue had, but she found a new center for her life in community activism, focused particularly on improving the quality of services in her own working-class neighborhood of

"I've always tried to live by what Mary McCleod Bethune said: 'You may not be able to go everywhere; you may not be able to do everything; you may not be able to be everybody. But by the grace of God, go somewhere; do something; be somebody.'"

Georganna Deas

Coney Island in Brooklyn. Although she had been supporting herself nearly all her adult life, she had often depended on various programs—subsidized day care, public housing, and public transportation—to make ends meet. Moreover, once she left Bellevue, she never again had a job with health insurance, so her local public hospital became a vital source of care. Reaching out from her own experience, Deas became a leading spirit in Coney Island PRIDE (Progressive Rainbow Independents for Developing Empowerment). This neighborhood alliance, drawn from half a dozen different ethnic groups, won many small battles to improve the community, and one major war: It was a leading participant in the coalition that finally defeated Mayor Rudolph Guliani's plan to privatize the public Coney Island Hospital.

Deas still lives in Coney Island, and she remains a center of energy in her community. If her life story reminds us of the many adversities that urban working women of color faced during the latter part of the twentieth century, it also reminds us how many women triumphed over those adversities thanks to their own indomitable spirit.

Recent Trends Regarding Women and Crime

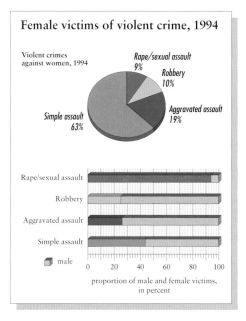

Female victims of violent crime, 1994

Violent crimes against women, 1994

Rape/sexual assault 9%

Robbery 10%

Aggravated assault 19%

Simple assault 63%

Rape/sexual assault

Robbery

Aggravated assault

Simple assault

male

0   20   40   60   80   100

proportion of male and female victims, in percent

Throughout American history, the great majority of women have experienced crime not as perpetrators but as victims. The decline of violent crime during the 1990s drew considerable attention, but the 1996 rate was still nearly double that of 1970, and more than 40 percent of these crimes were committed against women. The assumption that any woman walking alone at night was simply asking for trouble encouraged some women to study self-defense, while others organized rallies around the militant slogan: "Take Back the Night."

Yet for every woman who learned karate or joined a protest march, hundreds more accepted the double locks and the dependence on male escorts that went with trying to stay out of danger. Meanwhile, the fact that African-American women were victimized more frequently than white women highlighted the fact that women's vulnerability was influenced not only by their gender but also by their color, their class, and their neighborhood.

For most crimes, women's victimization rates were lower than men's, but in the category of rape, attempted rape, and sexual assault, women accounted for nine out of every 10 victims. Nearly 100,000 such crimes were reported to the

Forcible rapes, by state, 1996

Rate per 100,000 inhabitants

65.6
47.0
40.0
31.5
26.9
19.6

0   300 km

0   300 miles

police in 1996, giving the United States the highest reported rate of rape in the world. The actual prevalence may be considerably higher; the National Crime Victimization Survey estimated in 1995 that only about 30 percent of rapes were reported to the police.

Considering that such a large proportion of all crime victims were women, one might have expected women to be represented in equal numbers in law enforcement. However, in both the FBI and in local and state police forces, females accounted for only about one officer in 10 during the 1990s. When women first started joining police forces during the Progressive Era, many sought to orient police work toward a more social approach to crime, stressing counseling and prevention. Over time, however, these efforts were absorbed by other agencies, and policewomen, like their male colleagues, came to focus almost entirely on crime fighting.

Besides being crime victims and crime fighters, women were also crime suspects. More than 2 million women were arrested in 1996, about a quarter of them charged with violent crimes. Men still accounted for 80 percent of all arrests, however; the only two categories in which women outnumbered men were prostitution and runaways. As for imprisonment, women represented an even smaller proportion of prison inmates than of arrestees. But there were two troubling aspects in the pattern of female incarceration. One was the disproportionate number of African-American women in prison. The other was the doubling of female drug convictions between 1990 and 1996, which sparked a sharp rise in the number of women behind bars.

Women did not have to be arrested themselves to be affected by the rapid increase in incarcerations. Men were being imprisoned on a much vaster scale, and as the numbers of male inmates rose from about 300,000 in 1980 to more than 1 million in 1996, women all over the country—particularly low-income women and particularly African Americans—experienced the loss of husbands, lovers, sons, brothers, and fathers.

Drug use in female adults arrested in 21 cities, 1996	proportion tested positive, in percent
Manhattan, NY	83
Philadelphia, PA	81
Atlanta, GA	77
Portland, OR	74
Los Angeles, CA	74
St. Louis, MO	73
Indianapolis, IN	72
Cleveland, OH	70
Detroit, MI	69
Denver, CO	69
Fort Lauderdale, FL	66
Phoenix, AZ	65
San Diego, CA	62
Birmingham, AL	59
Washington, DC	58
Dallas, TX	58
Houston, TX	54
San Jose, CA	53
Omaha, NE	51
San Antonio, TX	44
New Orleans, LA	35

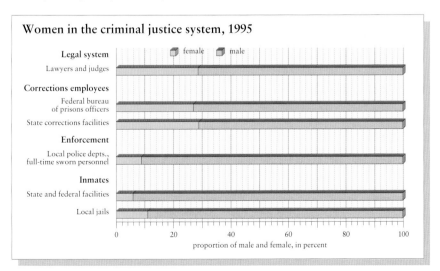

Women in the criminal justice system, 1995

Recent Trends in Women's Health

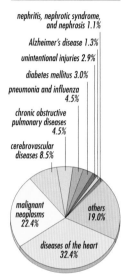

Causes of death for women, 1996

nephritis, nephrotic syndrome, and nephrosis 1.1%

Alzheimer's disease 1.3%

unintentional injuries 2.9%

diabetes mellitus 3.0%

pneumonia and influenza 4.5%

chronic obstructive pulmonary diseases 4.5%

cerebrovascular diseases 8.5%

malignant neoplasms 22.4%

others 19.0%

diseases of the heart 32.4%

Total number of deaths: 1,151,121

The years between 1900 and 1950 produced American history's most dramatic improvements in women's health, thanks to advances in public health, medicine, workplace safety, and the overall standard of living. The period from 1950 to 2000 brought less spectacular achievements, but women benefited from medical breakthroughs like antibiotics and the polio vaccine, as well as broader initiatives such as air pollution controls, tighter occupational safety regulations, campaigns against drunk driving, and the requirement for safety belts in cars. The importance of taking increased responsibility for one's health also received new attention, leading many women to stop smoking, limit their alcohol intake, pay closer attention to nutrition, get regular medical checkups, and exercise more frequently.

Childbirth used to be one of the most dangerous events in women's lives, killing thousands of women every year and leaving many more weakened for life. The progress made during the twentieth century can be seen in the statistics. In 1915, for every 100,000 live births, more than 600 mothers died in childbirth. By 1996 the number had dropped to six. This achievement reflected advances on many fronts: an overall improvement in mothers' levels of health and nutrition; the availability of antibiotics to stop infection; more consistent use of prenatal care; women's greater freedom to space their pregnancies through the use of contraceptives; and the legalization of abortion in 1973, which made it possible for women to end pregnancies without risking their own lives.

In the 1990s, heart disease and cancer were the two top killers of women, accounting for more than half of all female deaths. The case of heart disease—long a major cause of female mortality—highlights an important issue in women's health: for many years, medical approaches to this disease were based primarily on studies of male patients. Belatedly, it was learned that women's cardiac problems develop later in life, that their symptoms are dif-

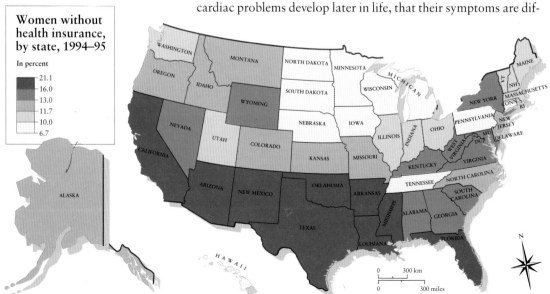

Women without health insurance, by state, 1994–95

In percent

- 21.1
- 16.0
- 13.0
- 11.7
- 10.0
- 6.7

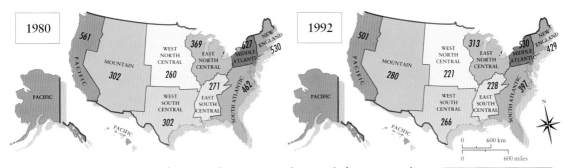

Abortion rate, by region, 1980 and 1992

260   number of abortions per 1,000 live births

ferent, and that a number of tests and treatments that work for men are less effective for women. These and other findings highlighted the danger of the long-standing assumption that research on men would provide all the information needed to understand women's diseases.

Perhaps the greatest problem in the women's health field in the 1990s was the question of inequality, particularly in terms of access to care. By 1996, more than 15 percent of American women had no health insurance. Others had access problems because the services they needed were located too far away, were scheduled at inconvenient times, or were not covered by their health insurance. These difficulties intersected with inequality related to race. Despite the advances in health care throughout the century, black women continued to have far higher infant mortality rates than white women, more low-birthweight babies, a higher death rate, a lower life expectancy, and nearly four times as many deaths in childbirth. In the case of AIDS, black women's infection rate was 20 times that of white women. The need for a more equitable system of care and for a clearer understanding of women's health needs represented two important goals for improving health in the twenty-first century.

New Life Fitness Center, Columbia, South Carolina

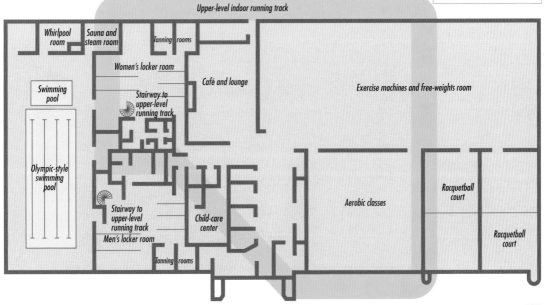

Living Longer

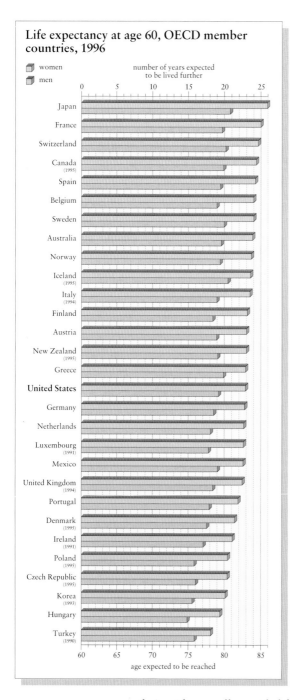

Life expectancy at age 60, OECD member countries, 1996

The emerging patterns of female health, work, and income discussed in the previous pages all helped shape what it meant to be an elderly woman in the United States at the end of the twentieth century. Advances in health paved the way, giving women longer lives than any previous generation had enjoyed. A baby girl born in 1900 had a life expectancy of only 48 years. By 1950, the number had climbed to 71, and in 1996 it was 79 (compared to 73 for men). Moreover, longer life expectancy did not simply mean more years of senility. By the end of the century, women in their seventies enjoyed a level of physical well-being that earlier generations of women had often lost in their forties. So great were the changes that at an age when older women used to start turning to their children for care, many were starting instead to care for their even older mothers.

For married women, there was one shadow over their extended lives—the fact that many of them could expect to outlive their husbands. By 1997, there were 6 million more women over 65 than men, and widows outnumbered widowers three to one. In earlier times, elderly widows often moved in with their children, but by the 1990s this had become far less common. Instead, such women were likely either to remain in the family home or move to one of the many apartment complexes that sprang up during these years to serve the elderly. At the end of the road lay the nursing home; by 1997, the nation contained almost 17,000 of these facilities, and about one out of every four American women over the age of 85 was living in one.

Trends in women's work and income helped determine the quality of their lives as they grew older. Husbands did not always leave their widows well provided for, and because women generally had less consistent and less well-paid careers, their own savings and retirement income were often limited. The result was that in 1997, more than one third of all elderly women (about two thirds of African Americans and Latinas) were living in or near poverty, while the rates for men in each group were much lower. Under

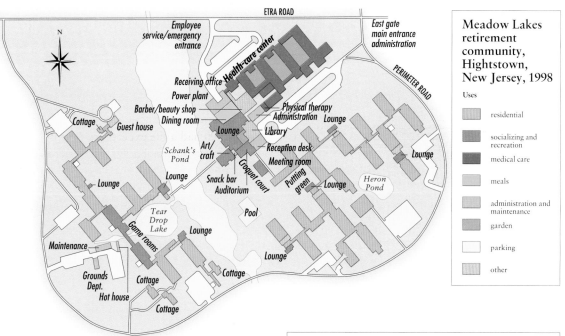

ETRA ROAD

Employee service/emergency entrance

East gate main entrance administration

PERIMETER ROAD

Receiving office — Health-care center

Power plant

Barber/beauty shop — Physical therapy
Dining room — Administration — Lounge

Cottage

Guest house

Lounge

Library

Schank's Pond

Art/craft — Reception desk

Croquet court — Meeting room

Lounge

Snack bar — Putting green — Lounge
Auditorium

Heron Pond

Lounge

Tear Drop Lake

Game rooms

Pool

Maintenance

Lounge

Lounge

Grounds Dept.

Cottage

Cottage

Hot house

Cottage

Meadow Lakes retirement community, Hightstown, New Jersey, 1998

Uses

- residential
- socializing and recreation
- medical care
- meals
- administration and maintenance
- garden
- parking
- other

these conditions, government programs played an important role in sustaining older women. Social Security, Supplemental Security Income, Medicare, and Medicaid did not eliminate female poverty, but they provided vital support, protecting poor women from destitution and giving all women a level of economic independence that women over 65 had rarely enjoyed in the past.

As women were living longer, they faced one great challenge: the need to make productive use of their added years. Throughout American history, women had faced many barriers, from physical ones such as mountains and deserts to mental ones such as race and class. Now women were ready to be pioneers of another kind, exploring how to make the most of a longer period of maturity than any previous generation had known.

Living arrangements and economic status of people aged 65 and over, 1990

women   men

	women	men
Married couples households	6	6
Living alone	26	17
Living with relatives	6	7
Living with nonrelatives	45	30
Group quarters or institutions	na	

percent in poverty

proportion of men and women in each kind of arrangement, in percent

0   10   20   30   40   50   60   70

Women aged 65 and over, by state, 1990

0   400 km
0   400 miles

ALASKA

HAWAII

Proportion of women aged 65 and over in the total female population, in percent

- 20.4
- 16.3
- 15.1
- 14.2
- 12.5
- 4.6

American Women: Statistics over Time

Female population of the United States by race and age

| | number of women | | | | percent distribution | | |
	total	white	black	other races	white	black	other races
1790	n/a	1,556,572	n/a	n/a	n/a	n/a	n/a
1800	-	2,111,141	.	.	.	.	.
1810	-	2,873,943	.	.	.	.	.
1820	4,741,848	3,870,988	870,860	-	81.6	18.4	-
1830	6,333,531	5,171,165	1,162,366	-	81.6	18.4	-
1840	8,380,921	6,940,261	1,440,660	-	82.8	17.2	-
1850	11,354,216	9,526,666	1,827,550	-	83.9	16.1	-
1860	15,358,117	13,111,150	2,225,086	21,881	85.4	14.5	0.1
1870	19,064,806	16,560,289	2,486,746	17,771	86.9	13.0	0.1
1880	24,636,963	21,272,070	3,327,678	37,215	86.3	13.5	0.2
1890	30,710,613	26,830,879	3,753,073	126,661	87.4	12.2	0.4
1900	37,243,479	32,622,949	4,447,539	172,991	87.6	11.9	0.5
1910	44,727,298	39,579,044	4,942,228	206,026	88.5	11.0	0.5
1920	51,935,452	46,421,794	5,253,890	259,768	89.4	10.1	0.5
1930	60,807,176	54,404,615	6,035,789	366,772	89.5	9.9	0.6
1940	65,815,399	58,819,215	6,596,652	399,532	89.4	10.0	0.6
1950	76,139,192	67,894,638	7,744,182	500,372	89.2	10.2	0.7
1960	90,991,681	80,464,583	9,758,423	768,675	88.4	10.7	0.8
1970	104,299,734	91,027,988	11,831,973	1,439,773	87.3	11.3	1.4
1980	116,492,644	96,686,289	13,975,836	5,830,519	83.0	12.0	5.0
1990	127,470,455	102,210,190	15,815,909	9,444,356	80.2	12.4	7.4

Older women

| | women 65 and over as % of | |
	total female population	total 65+ population
1870	3	50
1880	3	50
1890	4	49
1900	4	50
1910	4	50
1920	5	50
1920	5	50
1930	5	50
1940	7	51
1950	9	53
1960	10	55
1970	11	58
1980	13	60
1990	15	60

Life expectancy at birth by sex and race

| | white | | nonwhite | |
	male	female	male	female
1900	46.6	48.7	32.5	33.5
1910	48.6	52.0	33.8	37.5
1920	54.4	55.6	45.5	45.2
1930	59.7	63.5	47.3	49.2
1940	62.1	66.6	51.5	54.9
1950	66.5	72.2	59.1	62.9
1960	67.4	74.1	61.1	66.3
1970	68.0	75.6	61.3	69.4
1980	70.7	78.1	65.3	73.6
1990	72.7	79.4	67.0	75.2
1995	73.4	79.6	67.9	75.7

Infant mortality by race

	deaths in first year of life per 1,000 live births		
	total	white	nonwhite
1915	99.9	98.6	181.2
1925	71.7	68.3	110.8
1935	55.7	51.9	83.2
1945	38.3	35.6	57.0
1955	26.4	23.6	42.8
1965	24.7	21.5	40.3
1975	16.1	14.2	24.2
1985	10.6	9.3	15.8
1995	7.6	6.3	15.1

Maternal mortality by race

	maternal deaths per 100,000 live births		
	total	white	nonwhite
1915	608	601	1056
1925	647	603	1162
1935	582	531	946
1945	207	172	455
1955	47	33	130
1965	32	21	84
1975	13	9	29
1985	8	5	22
1995	6	4	21

Marriages and divorces

	per 1,000 population	
	marriages	divorces
1920	12.0	1.6
1925	10.3	1.5
1930	9.2	1.6
1935	10.4	1.7
1940	12.1	2.0
1945	12.2	3.5
1946	16.4	4.3
1947	13.9	3.4
1950	11.1	2.6
1955	9.3	2.3
1960	8.5	2.2
1965	9.3	2.5
1970	10.6	3.5
1975	10.0	4.8
1980	10.6	5.2
1985	10.1	5.0
1990	9.8	4.7
1995	7.6	4.1

Birthrate by race

	live births per 1,000 women aged 15–44 years		
	total	white	nonwhite
1800	n/a	278.0	n/a
1820	-	260.0	-
1840	-	222.0	-
1860	-	184.0	-
1880	-	155.0	-
1900	-	130.0	-
1910	126.8	123.8	-
1920	117.9	115.4	137.5
1930	89.2	87.1	105.9
1940	79.9	77.1	102.4
1945	85.9	83.4	106.0
1947	113.3	111.8	125.9
1950	106.2	102.3	137.3
1955	118.5	113.8	155.3
1960	118.0	113.2	153.6
1970	87.9	84.1	113.0
1980	68.4	64.8	84.7
1990	70.9	68.3	86.8
1995	65.6	64.4	72.3

Female-headed families

	female-headed as % of all families	poor female-headed families with children under 18 as % of all poor families with children
1940	11.2	n/a
1950	9.4	-
1960	10.0	27.7
1970	10.8	48.1
1980	14.6	56.1
1990	16.5	60.4
1995	17.6	60.8

Births to unmarried mothers

	unmarried births as % of total live births
1940	3.5
1950	3.9
1960	5.3
1970	10.7
1980	18.4
1990	28.0
1995	32.2

Female participation in the labor force

| | total | by marital status | | | working women as % of total labor force |
		single women	married women	widowed/ divorced	
1890	18.9	40.5	4.6	29.9	17.0
1900	20.6	43.5	5.6	32.5	18.1
1910	25.4	51.1	10.7	34.1	n/a
1920	23.7	46.4	9.0	n/a	20.4
1930	24.8	50.5	11.7	34.4	21.9
1940	27.4	48.1	14.7	32.0	25.2
1950	31.4	50.5	23.8	36.0	28.8
1960	34.8	44.1	30.5	37.1	32.3
1970	43.3	56.8	40.5	40.3	38.1
1980	51.5	64.4	49.9	43.6	42.5
1990	57.5	66.7	58.4	47.2	45.2
1995	58.9	66.8	61.0	47.4	46.1

Working mothers

	married women (husbands present) with children under 6 in the labor force, as % of all married women (husband present) with children under 6
1950	11.9
1955	16.2
1960	18.6
1965	23.3
1970	30.3
1975	36.7
1980	45.1
1985	53.4
1990	58.9
1995	63.5

Wage gap

	women's median earnings as % of men's
1951	63.9
1955	63.9
1960	60.7
1965	59.9
1970	59.4
1975	58.8
1980	60.2
1985	64.6
1990	71.6
1996	73.8

Degrees granted to women

| | bachelor's degrees | | doctoral degrees | |
	number	% of total	number	% of total
1870	1,378	14.7	0	n/a
1880	2,485	19.3	3	5.6
1890	2,682	17.3	2	1.3
1900	5,237	19.1	23	6.0
1910	8,437	22.7	44	9.9
1920	16,242	33.4	93	15.1
1930	48,869	39.9	353	15.4
1940	76,954	41.3	429	13.0
1950	103,217	23.9	643	9.7
1960	136,187	35.0	1,028	10.5
1970	343,060	41.5	3,976	13.3
1980	456,000	49.0	10,000	30.3
1990	560,000	53.2	14,000	36.8
1995	634,000	54.7	18,000	40.0

Women in U.S. Congress

| | number of women | | | % |
	senate	house	total	of full membership
1918	0	1	1	0.2
1922	1	3	4	0.8
1926	0	3	3	0.6
1930	0	9	9	1.7
1934	1	7	8	1.5
1938	2	6	8	1.5
1942	1	9	10	1.9
1946	0	11	11	2.1
1950	1	9	10	1.9
1954	2	11	13	2.4
1958	1	15	16	3.0
1962	2	18	20	3.8
1966	2	11	13	2.4
1970	1	10	11	2.1
1974	0	16	16	3.0
1978	2	18	20	3.7
1982	2	21	23	4.3
1986	2	23	25	4.7
1990	2	29	31	5.8
1994	7	47	54	10.1
1998	9	54	63	11.8

Voting in presidential elections by sex

| | % of voting age population who reported voting | | women as % of reported voters |
	women	men	
1964	67.0	71.9	51.1
1968	66.0	69.8	51.9
1972	62.0	64.1	52.3
1976	58.8	59.6	52.6
1980	59.4	59.1	53.0
1984	60.8	59.0	53.5
1988	58.3	56.4	53.3
1992	62.3	60.2	53.2
1996	55.5	52.8	53.4

Women in state legislatures

	number	percent of all legislators
1969	301	4.0
1971	344	4.5
1973	424	5.6
1975	604	8.0
1977	688	9.1
1979	770	10.3
1981	908	12.1
1983	991	13.3
1985	1103	14.8
1987	1170	15.7
1989	1270	17.0
1991	1368	18.3
1993	1524	20.5
1995	1532	20.6

Sources:
U.S. Bureau of the Census, *Historical Statistics of the United States, Colonial Times to 1970* (Washington, D.C.: U.S. Government Printing Office, 1975); U.S. Department of Commerce, *Statistical Abstract of the United States* (Washington, D.C.: U.S. Government Printing Office, annual); National Center for Health Statistics, *Health United States* (Hyattsville, MD: U.S. Government Printing Office, 1997 and 1998); Joseph Dalaker and Mary Naifeh, U.S. Bureau of the Census, Current Population Reports, Series P60–201, *Poverty in the United States: 1997* (Washington, D.C.: U.S. Government Printing Office, 1998); U.S. Women's Bureau, U.S. Department of Labor, *Equal Pay: A Thirty-Five Year Perspective* (Washington, D.C.: U.S. Government Printing Office, 1998); Center for American Women and Politics, Rutgers University. Calculations by the author.

Notes:
Infant mortality: Until 1980, rates were calculated based on the race of the child; since then, they have been based on the race of the mother. Nonwhite rate in 1995 is for black only.
Maternal mortality: Nonwhite rate 1985–95 is for black only.
Birthrate: From 1980 on, nonwhite rate is for black only.
Labor participation: Includes persons 15 and over from 1890–1930, 14 and over from 1940–60, 16 and over from 1970–95. From 1940 on, "married women" includes only women with husbands present.
Wage gap: Annual earnings for year-round full-time workers, based on real dollars calculated using the CPI-U with 1982–84 = 100. Persons 14 and older from 1951–79, 15 and older thereafter.

Further Reading

General and reference

Anderson, Karen, *Changing Woman: A History of Racial Ethnic Women in Modern America*, Oxford University Press, 1996.

Berkin, Carol Ruth, and Mary Beth Norton, *Women of America: A History*, Houghton Mifflin, 1979.

Brumberg, Joan Jacobs, *The Body Project: An Intimate History of American Girls*, Vintage Books, 1997.

Cullen-DuPont, Kathryn, *The Encyclopedia of Women's History in America*, Facts on File, 1996.

Evans, Sara M., *Born for Liberty: A History of Women in America*, Free Press, 1997.

Faderman, Lillian, *Odd Girls and Twilight Lovers: A History of Lesbian Life in Twentieth-Century America*, Columbia University Press, 1991.

Flexner, Eleanor, and Ellen Fitzpatrick, *Century of Struggle: The Woman's Rights Movement in the United States*, enlarged ed., Harvard University Press, 1996.

Foner, Philip S., *Women and the American Labor Movement: From the First Trade Unions to the Present*, Free Press, 1982.

Gordon, Linda, *Pitied But Not Entitled: Single Mothers and the History of Welfare*, Harvard University Press, 1994.

Gordon, Linda, *Woman's Body, Woman's Right: A Social History of Birth Control in America*, Grossman, 1976.

Heinemann, Sue, *Timelines of American Women's History*, Berkley
Publishing, 1996.

Hine, Darlene Clark, *A Shining Thread of Hope: The History of Black
Women in America*, Broadway Books, 1998.

Holm, Maj. Gen. Jeanne, *Women in the Military: An Unfinished Revolution*,
rev. ed., Presidio Press, 1992.

Hymowitz, Carol, and Michaele Weissman, *A History of Women in America*,
Bantam, 1978.

Jones, Jacqueline, *Labor of Love, Labor of Sorrow: Black Women, Work,
and the Family from Slavery to the Present*, Basic Books, 1985.

Kessler-Harris, Alice, *Out to Work: A History of Wage-Earning Women in
America*, Oxford University Press, 1992.

Mankiller, Wilma et al., eds., *The Reader's Companion to U.S. Women's
History*, Houghton Mifflin, 1998.

Matthews, Glenna, *The Rise of Public Woman: Woman's Power and Woman's
Place in the United States, 1630–1970*, Oxford University Press, 1992.

Niethammer, Carolyn, *Daughters of the Earth: The Lives and Legends of
American Indian Women*, Touchstone Books, 1996.

Peiss, Kathy, *Hope in a Jar: The Making of America's Beauty Culture*,
Metropolitan Books, 1998.

Ruiz, Vicki L., *From Out of the Shadows: Mexican Women in Twentieth-
Century America*, Oxford University Press, 1998.

Shoemaker, Nancy, *Negotiators of Change: Historical Perspectives on Native American Women*, Routledge, 1995.

Scott, Anne Firor, *Natural Allies: Women's Associations in American History*, University of Illinois Press, 1991.

Sherr, Lynn, and Jurate Kazickas, *Susan B. Anthony Slept Here: A Guide to American Women's Landmarks*, Times Books, 1994.

Solomon, Barbara, *In the Company of Educated Women: A History of Women and Higher Education in America*, Yale University Press, 1985.

Strasser, Susan, *Never Done: A History of American Housework*, Pantheon, 1982.

Taeuber, Cynthia M., ed., *Statistical Handbook on Women in America*, 2d ed., Oryx Press, 1996.

Tilly, Louise A., and Patricia Gurin, eds., *Women, Politics, and Change*, Russell Sage, 1990.

Ware, Susan, ed., *Modern American Women: A Documentary History*, 2d ed., McGraw-Hill, 1996.

Woloch, Nancy, ed. *Early American Women: A Documentary History, 1600–1900*, 2d ed., McGraw-Hill, 1996.

Books about specific periods

Berkin, Carol, *First Generations: Women in Colonial America*, Hill and Wang, 1996.

Chafe, William H., *The American Woman: Her Changing Social, Economic, and Political Roles, 1920–1970*, Oxford University Press, 1972.

Davis, Flora, *Moving the Mountain: The Women's Movement in America Since 1960*, University of Illinois Press, 1999.

Dreiser, Theodore, *Sister Carrie*, Penguin Books, 1986.

Evans, Sara, *Personal Politics: The Roots of Women's Liberation in the Civil Rights Movement and the New Left*, Alfred A. Knopf, 1979.

Fox-Genovese, Elizabeth, *Within the Plantation Household: Black and White Women of the Old South*, University of North Carolina Press, 1988.

Katzman, David, *Seven Days a Week: Women and Domestic Service in Industrializing America*, University of Illinois Press, 1981.

May, Elaine Tyler, *Homeward Bound: American Families in the Cold War Era*, Basic Books, 1988.

Myres, Sandra L., *Westering Women and the Frontier Experience, 1800–1915*, University of New Mexico Press, 1982.

Smith-Rosenberg, Carroll, *Disorderly Conduct: Visions of Gender in Victorian America*, Oxford University Press, 1985.

Stansell, Christine, *City of Women: Sex and Class in New York, 1789–1860*, University of Illinois Press, 1987.

Tax, Meredith, *The Rising of the Women: Feminist Solidarity and Class Conflict, 1880–1917*, Monthly Review Press, 1980.

Ulrich, Laurel Thatcher, *A Midwife's Tale: The Life of Martha Ballard, Based on Her Diary, 1785–1812*, Alfred A. Knopf, 1990.

Index

Map Acknowledgments

Most of the maps in this atlas are based on multiple sources, or on information from the federal government, particularly the Census Bureau and the Department of Labor. Other sources are listed below.

Pages

16–17   Roy S. Dickens, Jr., *Cherokee Prehistory*, University of Tennessee Press, 1976.

18–20   James W. Clay et al., *Land of the South*, Oxmoor, 1989; Sumner Chilton Powell, *Puritan Village*, Wesleyan University Press, 1963.

22–23   Allan Kullikoff, *Tobacco and Slaves*, University of North Carolina Press, 1986.

24–25   Rhys Isaac, *Transformation of Virginia*, University of North Carolina Press, 1982; Allan Kullikoff, *Tobacco and Slaves*, University of North Carolina Press, 1986.

30–31   Laurel Thatcher Ulrich, *A Midwife's Tale*, Vintage Books, 1990.

36–37   Helen Hornbeck Tanner, ed., *Atlas of Greak Lakes Indian History*, University of Oklahoma Press, 1986.

38–39   Paul E. Johnson, *A Shopkeeper's Millennium*, Hill and Wang, 1978; Oscar Handlin, Boston's Immigrants, rev. ed., Harvard University Press, 1979.

40–41   *Proceedings of the Women's Rights Convention*, Akron, OH, May 1851.

42–43   John Michael Vlach, *Back of the Big House*, University of North Carolina Press, 1993; New York Public Library.

44–45   Kenneth T. Jackson, ed., *Atlas of American History*, Scribner's, 1978.

46–47   Kathryn Kish Sklar and Thomas Dublin, *Women and Power in American History*, v. 1, Prentice Hall, 1991.

50–51   *The Sanitary Commission of the United States Army*, U.S. Sanitary Commission, 1864; Charles J. Stillé, *History of the United States Sanitary Commission*, Lippincott, 1866; Frederick H. Dyer, ed., *Compendium of the War of the Rebellion*, v. 1, Yoseloff, 1959.

54–55   Laura Josephine Webster, "Operation of the Freedmen's Bureau in South Carolina," *Smith College Studies in History*, v. 1 (January 1916); David C. Barrow, Jr., "A Georgia Plantation," *Scribner's Monthly*, 21 (1881).

56–57   Gavin Wright, *Old South, New South*, Basic Books, 1986; Historic Stagville, Durham, N.C.

58–59   North Dakota Historical Society; Adriance Memorial Library, Poughkeepsie, N.Y.

60–61   Andrew Jackson Downing, *Victorian Cottage Residences*, rev. ed., Dover, 1981 (orig. 1873).

62–63   William M. DeMarco, *Ethnics and Enclaves*, UMI Research Press, 1989.

64–65   David Ward, *Poverty, Ethnicity, and the American City, 1840–1925*, Cambridge University Press, 1989.

68–69   Susan L. Porter, ed., *Women of the Commonwealth*, University of Massachusetts Press, 1996.

70–71   Ardis Cameron, *Radicals of the Worst Sort*, University of Illinois Press, 1995.

72–73   Theodore Dreiser, *Sister Carrie*, Penguin, 1981; Joanne Meyerowitz, *Women Adrift*, University of Chicago Press, 1988.

74–75   Annie Nathan Meyer, ed., *Woman's Work in America*, Holt, 1891.

76–77   Dolores Hayden, *The Grand Domestic Revolution*, MIT Press, 1981; Elizabeth Lindsay Davis, *The Story of the Illinois Federation of Colored Women's Clubs*, Hall, 1997 (orig. 1922).

84–85   Dorothy and Carl J. Schneider, *Into the Breach*, Viking, 1991; Ida Clyde Clarke, *American Women and the World War*, Appleton, 1918.

86–87   *Thirty Years of Lynching in the United States*, Arno Press, 1969.

88–89   Harriet A. Byrne and Cecile Hillyer, *Unattached Women on Relief in Chicago, 1937*, U.S. Goverment Printing Office, 1938.

90–91   Jacquelyn Dowd Hall, *Like a Family*, University of North Carolina Press, 1987; Gendolyn Salisbury Hughes, *Mothers in Industry*, New Republic, 1925.

92–93   Julie A. Matthei, *An Economic History of Women in America*, Schocken, 1982; Ronald C. Tobey, *Technology as Freedom*, University of California Press, 1996; James J. Flink, *The Automobile Age*, MIT Press, 1988.

94–95   *Film Daily Yearbook of Motion Pictures* (1924).

96–97   Harriet A. Byrne, *Women Unemployed Seeking Relief in 1933*, U.S. Goverment Printing Office, 1936.

98–99   "My Day" typescripts, F.D.R. Presidential Library

100–1   Women's Army Corps Foundation.

102–3   Constance Green, "The Role of Women as Production Workers in War Plants in the Connecticut Valley," *Smith College Studies in History*, 1946; Lowell Juilliard Carr and James Edson Stermer, *Willow Run*, Harper, 1952; Philip Funigiello, *The Challenge to Urban Liberalism*, University of Tennessee Press, 1978; Richard S. Nishimoto, *Inside an American Concentration Camp*, University of Arizona Press, 1995.

104–5   Barbara Mae Kelly, "The Politics of House and Home" (Ph.D. diss.), UMI Research Press, 1988; Brian J.L. Berry, Chicago: *Transformations of an Urban System*, Lehman, 1976.

110–11 Gerald Pomper, *Voters' Choice*, Rutgers University Press, 1975.

114, 118 Reynolds Farley, *The New American Reality*, Russell Sage, 1996.

120–21 Center for the American Woman and Politics, Rutgers University.

126–27 Institute for Women's Policy Research, *The Status of Women in the States, 1998–99*, New Life Fitness World, Columbia, South Carolina

128–29 Meadow Lakes Retirement Community; *OECD in Figures: Statistics on Member Countries*, 1998 ed.

Acknowledgments

Pictures are reproduced by permission of, or have been provided by the following:

Arcadia Editions Limited: 16, 42
British Library: 62
Brown Brothers: 15, 40
Denver Public Library: 33
Historic New Orleans Collection: 24
Hulton Deutsch: 53
Library of Congress: 10, 81
MPI/Bettman Archive: 98
National Archives: 13, 51, 75
New York Times: 109
Peter Newarks American Pictures: 37
Schlesinger Library: 78
Wide World Photo, Dorothea Lange: 96

Design: Malcolm Swanston, Elsa Gibert.

Cartography: Elsa Gibert with
 Peter Gamble, Peter A.B. Smith, Malcolm Swanston.

Drawings: Peter A.B. Smith.